SCRAPPLIQUÉ

Scrappliqué (skrap-li-kay) — the creative art of making items from scraps of fabric. The process of transforming unused fabric into apparel and home decorating items.

SCRAPPLIQUÉ

Jean Marshall

Sterling Publishing Co., Inc. New York
A Sterling/Chapelle Book

Chapelle, Ltd.:
 Jo Packham
 Sara Toliver
 Cindy Stoeckl

 Editor: Ray Cornia
 Editorial Director: Caroll Shreeve
 Art Director: Karla Haberstich
 Graphic Illustrator: Kim Taylor
 Copy Editor: Marilyn Goff

 Staff: Burgundy Alleman, Areta Bingham, Susan Jorgensen,
  Emily Kirk, Barbara Milburn, Lecia Monsen, Karmen Quinney,
  Desirée Wybrow

If you have any questions or comments, please contact:
Chapelle, Ltd., Inc., P.O. Box 9252, Ogden, UT 84409
 (801) 621-2777 • (801) 621-2788 Fax
 e-mail: chapelle@chapelleltd.com
 web site: www.chapelleltd.com

Designed by Tracy Merrill

Every effort has been made to ensure that all information in this book is accurate. However, due to dif-
fering conditions, tools, and individual skills, the publisher cannot be responsible for any injuries, losses,
and/or other damages which may result from the use of the information in this book.

This volume is meant to stimulate decorating ideas. If readers are unfamiliar or not
proficient in a skill necessary to attempt a project, we urge they refer to an instructional book specifically
addressing the required technique.

Library of Congress Cataloging-in-Publication Data

Jean, Marshall.
  Scrappliqué (skrap-li-kay) : the creative art of making items from
scraps of fabric, the process of transforming unused fabric into apparel
and home decorating itmes / [Jean Marshall].
       p. cm.
  Includes index.
  ISBN 1-4027-0001-6
 1. Textile crafts. 2. Household linens. 3. Wearable art. I. Title:
Scrappliqué. II. Title.
TT699.J43 2003
746.46'043--dc21

                                           2002154364

10 9 8 7 6 5 4 3 2 1

Published by Sterling Publishing Co., Inc.
387 Park Avenue South, New York, NY 10016
©2003 by Jean Marshall
Distributed in Canada by Sterling Publishing
⅝ Canadian Manda Group, One Atlantic Avenue, Suite 105
Toronto, Ontario, Canada M6K 3E7
Distributed in Great Britain by Chrysalis Books
64 Brewery Road, London N7 9NT, England
Distributed in Australia by Capricorn Link (Australia) Pty. Ltd.
P.O. Box 704, Windsor, NSW 2756, Australia
Printed and Bound in China
All Rights Reserved

Sterling ISBN 1-4027-0001-6

MONDAY

Introduction

SCRAPPLIQUÉ (skrap-li-kay)

What's this? No, you won't find this word in the dictionary, but you will find its meaning if you look up SCRAP (small detached piece, the least bit) and APPLIQUÉ—from the French—(to put on; a cutout decoration fastened to a larger piece of material; to apply as a decoration or an ornament to a larger surface).

The Refrigerator Approach

Haven't you gone to the refrigerator and stared inside thinking, "What can I make with left-over cooked potatoes and some carrots and two frozen chicken breasts?" You might come up with potato salad, rice cooked with shredded carrot and the chicken breasts warmed in a sauce of cream of chicken soup and a dollop of cooking sherry. Or you might cut up the carrots, steam them, add the chopped up potatoes, cut the chicken into tiny bites, throw in some chicken broth and a bay leaf as well as some tiny pasta and make a tasty soup. I'm sure you could come up with many other possibilities.

Now, this left-over approach might be taken with your fabric cache. "What can I make with a half yard of an upholstery remnant?" you may ask. Or "What scraps can I cover this binder with to create an interesting photo album?" You might decide to embellish a scrap of velveteen with beads, or stitch on a photo transferred to fabric, etc. Or "What am I going to do with all these odds and ends of ribbon?" Make an evening bag? A sachet? A book cover? A doll? A greeting card? Or all of the above?

Adapt the Projects to Your Vision

The expectation is not that you recreate the projects in this book exactly—though I will tell you exactly what I did. However, you may take ideas from *Scrappliqué,* then look at your "scraps" and create adaptations of these projects to make use of what you have to suit your own style. Well, okay, you can fudge and go buy a piece of this or that, but the truth is that most of the projects in this book were made from "scraps" on hand. Does that indicate the congested state my sewing room is in?

One last quick note, since this book was written for people who have sewn before, normal sewing tools and generally understood sewing operations are not explained in great detail. However, I have tried to include enough detail so anyone can easily follow the steps required to successfully complete any of the projects included in this book. I have also tried to include a wide variety of projects for use in different decorating applications and styles—but most of all, I wanted to share the joy I've found through sewing.

Jean Marshall

Contents

Contents

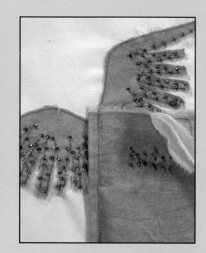

Eclectic (e-klek-tik) Scrappliqué — selecting
what is most pleasing and interesting in
various methods or styles; mixing elements
of whatever appeals to your individual
sense of design.

Eclectic Scrappliqué

Nostalgia Piece

Supplies:

Cheesecloth

Craft glue

Old photographs

Old-style wooden clothespins without hinges (There is a smaller pin called a baby flat that is just right. The miniature ones are too small.)

Old washboard

Photo heat transfers

Three screw eyes

Twine

My mother saved the washboard she used for the first few years of her marriage in the early 1940s. I "borrowed" it and scoured her albums for photos of our family and the house we lived in when I was a toddler.

Instructions:

1. After taking your photographs and making photo-copies the size you wish, play with the arrangement across the washboard. An odd number works best. Try two on the top and three below. When you are satisfied with your photo placement and size, have heat transfers made of the photocopies. Trim the transfers so they have ¼" or ½" white borders.

2. Cut out cheesecloth pieces larger than the transfer images, 2" larger at the top and 1" to 1½" larger at the sides and bottom. Cut a curve between the top two corners and echo that curved line below as if the fabric were drooping on the clothesline. Center each transfer photo on cheesecloth piece and using a long stitch, sew it ⅛" from the edge of the photo.

3. Place a screw eye in the upper-left, upper-right, and lower-right corners of the washboard. Tie one length of twine to screw eye at upper left, pull it firmly to the eye at upper right, and tie in place. Tie the second length of twine at upper left as well, but pull it firmly to tie at lower right. Trim the ends.

4. With a small drop of craft glue, attach the corners of the cheesecloth photos to the twine. When dry, add the clothespins.

Tip: Heat-transfer material can be purchased at craft or fabric stores. Follow manufacturer's instructions.

Quotable Curtain

Supplies:

Light-colored cotton
fabric strips

Photo heat transfers

T-square

White lightweight
cotton fabric

*Tip: You may want to dye
the fabric strips on which
you will place the text.
You can use commercial
dyes that are available in
craft, fabric, or grocery
stores or use natural dyes
such as tea, coffee, onion
skins, or cranberries.*

The open shelves in my study looked so untidy that I
hung a rod and curtain there. It is a small room with
white walls, so to keep the room light, I planned a white
curtain with appliqués on it of some of the quotes that I
like about books and reading. The peach and mauve colors in the curtain relate to the kilim on the floor. Unlike
gathered curtains, this one is only as wide as the space,
so when the curtain is opened it is flat and the quotes
can be read.

Instructions:

1. Measure the length and width to be covered by the
   curtain. Add 1½" to each side, 2½" to the top, and 3½"
   to the bottom. Cut the fabric to these dimensions.

2. Press all edges under ½". Press the top under 2", sides
   1", bottom 3", and sew around all inside edges.

3. Choose quotes. Enlarge them on the computer or at a
   copy shop. Make quotes large enough to be seen
   some distance away. Lay paper copies of the text on
   the curtain to plan your layout. Draw a map to keep
   the design in mind.

4. Tear strips of fabric to accommodate each line of text,
   leaving ¼" or so above and below the letters. I liked
   the torn raw edges.

   *Note: If you want to turn edges under for a neater look,
   allow an additional ¼" seam allowance on all sides.*

5. Have heat transfers made on light-colored cotton
   strips—or—buy an inexpensive stencil set and trace
   the words on fabric with a fabric pen or a pencil and
   fill in with acrylic paint combined with textile medium.

(Continued on page 14)

Literature is the lie that tells the truth.

Dorothy Allison

The dark night was the first book of poetry,
and the constellations were the poems.

Chet Raymo

There is a land

Of magic folks and deed.

And anyone

Can visit there

Who reads and reads and reads.

Leland B. Jacobs

My library was dukedom enough.

William Shakespeare

You may have tangible wealth untold:

Caskets of jewels and coffers of gold.

Richer than I you can never be —

I had a Mother who read to me.

Strickland Gillialan

The habit of reading is the only enjoyment in which there is no alloy; it lasts

when all other pleasures fade.

Anthony Trollope

(Continued from page 12)

6. Using a T-square to keep lines straight, mark your layout with a pencil. Lay out the printed strips so the bottom edge just covers the pencil line. Pin securely in place. Machine-sew each strip to the curtain, using the longest stitch setting.

7. To attach curtain to rod, you can sew small button holes across the top hem and use shower curtain rings, or you can use traditional curtain rings and rods.

Tip: Using shower curtain rings is an easy and economical yet interesting touch to finish your design.

Tip: The design elements on your curtain can have special meaning to you. Add only dimensional aspects that are not too heavy or bulky.

Tip: Embellishments need not always be sewn down with finished edges. This primitive treatment with raw edges is more appropriate for this artist's interpretation.

Supplies:

Beads and charms
(optional)

Fabric glue

Fabric-paint pen

Organza strip: 5" x 14"

Permanent or fabric ink

Photo heat transfers

Potpourri or lavender

Ribbons: ¼"–4" wide,
1"–6" long

Rubber stamps

Scraps of fabrics: satins,
silks, taffetas, velvets,
etc.

Scrap of muslin: 1¼" x 6"

Fresh sachets can be made for a gift or for personal use
to make your life a little nicer.

Instructions:

Sachet I: Organza

1. Fold short ends of organza strip together and crease.

2. On one half of organza, sew a strip of wide ribbon
   lengthwise.

3. Tear a strip of fabric upon which you have handwrit-
   ten, using fabric-paint pen, or heat-transferred a
   phrase you have chosen.

4. Overlap the bottom edge of the text on the top edge
   of the wide ribbon.

5. Straight-stitch ⅛" in along both long edges of fabric.

6. Stitch a piece of rose ribbon inside the left edge of the
   overlapped ribbons.

   *Optional: You may embellish this appliqué with seeds
   and/or a tiny charm.*

7. Fold organza with wrong sides together and sew ¼" in
   along the two sides, leaving the top open.

8. Turn, press, and sew ¼" in again. Turn and press.

9. Add dried lavender or your choice of potpourri.

(Continued on page 18)

Sachet I

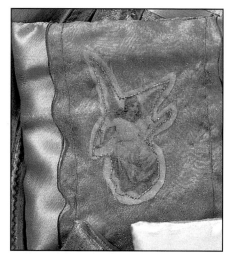

Sachet II

Sachet III

(Continued from page 16)

10. Tuck open edges inside and stitch closed by hand or machine.

    Optional: Stitch a ribbon loop to one corner for placing on a hanger.

Sachet II: Gossamer over images

1. Follow Step 1 on page 16 for the bag, except use a piece of satin, taffeta, or silk instead of organza.

2. With a dab of fabric glue, apply an image to the front of the bag. (An image clipped from a print scrap or one you have heat-transferred onto fabric.)

3. Lay a piece of gossamer wire-edged ribbon the height of the bag over the image. Sew a straight line down each edge. Sew through the gossamer around the image underneath ⅛" in from the edges.

    Note: Metallic thread is nice to use for this application.

4. Follow Steps 7–10 on page 16 and above for finishing the bag.

Sachet III: Rubber stamp images

1. You can use rubber stamps and fabric ink or permanent ink to stamp an image onto a small rectangle of satin or organza before stitching to front of bag as shown in photo at left.

    Optional: You may use scraps of satin or taffeta to make half-sized sachet bags. You may use organza for the back and satin for the front or vice versa. You may choose to machine-stitch a piece to the front of the bag, leaving raw edges, or turn them under ⅛", press, and stitch by hand or machine. Metallic thread adds interest as do embellishments such as beads, buttons, charms, or sequins.

Hand Towel

Supplies:

Linen hand towel

Silk ribbons: gold, green, 7mm

Flower Pattern
Enlarge 200%

It is easy to make a fancy hand towel with colored ribbon. These attractive towels will not only make your guest bath special, they also make very nice gifts.

Instructions:

1. Transfer Flower Pattern onto the towel.

2. Cut green ribbon to fit along stem and leaf lines. Allow an extra ¼" at each end to tuck under.

3. Tuck the bottom end of the ribbon under and lay the center of the ribbon on the stem line. Fold the top into a point. Sew down the center of the ribbon.

4. Repeat the process of laying the green ribbon along the pattern lines and sewing down the center line for the leaves.

5. Start at the center of the flower pattern and lay the gold ribbon on the line and slowly sew along the center of the ribbon along the pattern lines. Fold the end under at the top of the flower.

6. Fold the flower ribbon toward the center of the flower to create a ruffle effect.

Oriental Pillow

Supplies:

Fabric glue

Metallic paints: bronze, copper

Oriental tassel with ornate medallion

Paintbrush

Polyester stuffing

Silk and velvet fabrics in shades of purple

A little something from the orient has always seemed exotic to me. This little pillow in royal purple adds a zest of intrigue to my room, and can be placed anywhere.

Instructions:

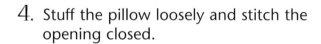

1. Sew velvet and silk together to form an 8" square.

2. Use brush and metallic paints to lightly paint a 3" circle in the center of the top half, and a square in the bottom half of the square. Allow the fabric to show through in places. Let dry.

3. Cut another piece of silk the same size as the front. Place right sides together and sew around edges, leaving an opening for stuffing.

4. Stuff the pillow loosely and stitch the opening closed.

5. Wrap the cord around the pillow and secure the ends at center of circle with fabric glue.

6. With fabric glue, adhere the medallion to the center of the painted circle, leaving the tassel free.

Tip: You can fill the pillow with an oriental-blend sachet to increase the allure of this elegant piece. Herbs such as basil, chamomile, sage, sweet flag, rosemary, tansy, or woodruff work well.

Portrait Pillow Top

Eclectic Scrappliqué Design

Designed by Jenni Christensen

Supplies:

Beads

Cloth napkin: 18" sq.

Fabric squares to layer the pillow front several times

Fusing tape or webbing

Light-colored background fabric

Photo heat transfer

Pillow form: 18" sq.

Scraps of fabrics and ribbons

Silk flowers and leaves

Trims: fringes, piping, upholstery, about 2 yds. each

Two pieces velveteen or upholstery fabric for pillow front and back: 19" sq.

I like the feel of custom or one-of-a-kind decorating items. A pillow with a portrait of a special family member is just perfect to give your room that custom flair.

Instructions:

1. Select a photo (I like black-and-whites) of the person you want as the focus of the pillow.

2. Heat-transfer the photo to a light-colored background fabric piece.

(Continued on page 23)

Detail of fabric layers and silk flower decoration

(Continued from page 21)

3. Using a fusing tape or webbing, fuse the image onto the cloth napkin. This will be the first layer. Bead around the edges of the photo transfer.

   Note: Gather together trims, beads, silk flowers, etc., that remind you of the person in the photo.

4. Attach the first layer (photo transfer) to the pillow front—or attach several layers of fabric, each slightly larger than the layer on top of it, again embellishing with beading or decorative stitching to make the pillow more elaborate.

5. Pull apart silk flowers and leaves. Select those you would like to use as embellishment and press flat.

6. Pin or tack down trims and flower shapes as you like. Continue beading and sewing around the photo on pillow top until it is full of embellishment. Add more layers of fabric as desired.

7. Select fringe or piping and include it in the seam as you sew the front to the back—right sides together—leaving one side open. Trim corners and turn.

8. Insert pillow form and hand-stitch the open side closed.

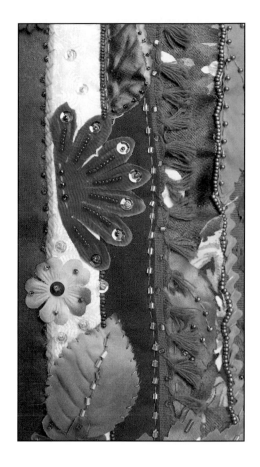

Photos illustrate beadwork, stitching, layering, and various types of accent embellishment

Star Pillow

Supplies:

Fabric glue

Pillow form: 18"

Scraps of embroidered paisley fabrics in at least two colors

Silk: ½ yd.

Dark base fabric: stiff, heavy, 19" sq.

In India, scarves and head coverings are lavishly embroidered, sometimes so much that the ground fabric is hard to see. This elaborate pillow follows that motif.

Instructions:

1. Use Star Pattern below to lay out first embroidered fabric and make a four-armed star.

   Note: It may be necessary to piece the scraps to get the shape and the patterns to align.

2. Sparingly glue the star onto the center of the base fabric.

   Note: Do not glue all the way out to the edges to allow the star to overlap the edges of the other embroidered fabric triangles.

3. Fill in the triangles formed around the star with a second embroidered fabric. Slip the edges of the triangles underneath the edges of the star. Glue in place onto the base fabric.

   Note: Again, you may have to piece the fabrics to make the designs fit the space.

4. Cut two strips from embroidered fabric or ribbon approximately 1"-wide for each side of the pillow. Adhere these strips onto the base fabric to make a border.

5. Cut the silk to match the size of the top for the back. Sew the top and back with right sides together, leaving an opening for the pillow form. Turn.

6. Insert the pillow form and stitch the opening closed.

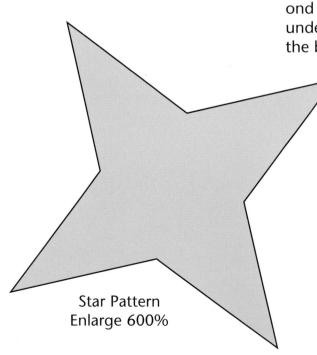

Star Pattern
Enlarge 600%

Joy Pillow

Eclectic Scrappliqué Design

Supplies:

Contrasting and coordinating colored threads including metallic threads

Embroidery hoop

Fabric-paint pens

Grosgrain ribbon: 1" x ½ yd.

Metal star charm

Plastic beads for filling

Satin for backing: 8" sq.

Scraps of felts: cream, orange

Scraps of fabrics and ribbons

Water-soluble stabilizer material: 11" sq.

Every now-and-again, I find something that I really enjoy and want to share with others. This project is just plain joyful. A joy to make, a joy to have, and a joy to play with. That's why I call this my Joy Pillow.

Instructions:

1. Measure and mark a 5" square in the center of the stabilizer. Place the stabilizer in an embroidery hoop and stretch tight.

2. Cut up the ribbons, fabrics, and threads into confetti-sized pieces.

3. Following manufacturer's instructions, set up for machine embroidery.

4. Place the embroidery hoop under the sewing machine needle. Lay the ribbon, fabric, and thread pieces on the stabilizer. Begin to sew in a vermiculate pattern over the ribbon, fabric, and thread pieces. Continue to add pieces and sew down until the marked off area and approximately ¼" past the marked area is covered.

   NOTE: For a lacy effect, leave some of the cut material loose and bouncy by not sewing it completely down—however, there must be something sewn down beneath the material left loose. Anywhere the stabilizer shows will leave a hole.

5. Remove the square from the hoop. Immerse and dissolve the stabilizer in cool water, following manufacturer's instructions. You have made a piece of ribbon fabric. Allow to dry.

26

6. Cut a 1¾" square from the cream felt and a 2½" square from the orange felt. Trace the Joy Pattern at right onto the cream felt with a dark fabric-paint pen.

7. Place the cream felt on the orange felt and sew around the edge of the cream felt. Place the felt pieces in the center of the ribbon fabric and sew around the edge of the orange felt.

8. Sew over the traced "JOY" with the machine.

9. Color around and inside the "JOY" with fabric-paint pens, blending the colors together.

10. Measure the side edges of the ribbon fabric. Cut two pieces from grosgrain ribbon to fit and sew along the side edges. Repeat for the top and bottom edges, overlapping the completed side edges.

11. With right sides together, sew the backing fabric around edges of the grosgrain ribbon, leaving 1½" opening for turning. Clip the corners and trim if necessary. Turn and stuff the pillow with plastic beads.

12. Slip-stitch the opening completely closed.

Joy Pattern

Christmas Coat

Supplies:

For coat
Cream brocade (Refer to pattern requirements.)

Commercial pattern for infant coat

Embellishments: bugle beads, feather, gold needle, gold thread, gold trims, lace, rhinestones, star sequins

Fabric dove

Gold lamé: 1 yd.

Satin lining: blue, cream

Scraps of fabrics

For moon
Angel transfers

Brocade: ¼ yd.

Charms: moon, stars, sun

Polyester stuffing

Scraps of ribbons

For a Christmas exhibit, I created a tiny wearable-art coat of brocades and angel transfers. Part of the binding is unsewn with a white feather peeking out and gold needle with gold thread in the midst of a stitch. Perhaps the angels were not finished with their gifts when the star appeared. A wreath of sun, moon, and star using the same techniques, would also be appropriate gifts for a "newborn king."

Instructions:

Making the coat

1. Cut one coat from brocade and one from blue satin (to use as a lining).

2. Cut cream satin to create a yoke at the top of the right and left fronts. They may be different lengths. For the back, cut a v-shaped yoke.

3. Appliqué the cream satin to the brocade coat front.

4. Enlarge the Christmas Coat Patterns on page 31, and trace the Star pattern onto the right front. Stitch on lines with silver thread.

5. Place three angel transfers down the left front and sew around edges, followed by a frame of ribbon.

6. Using the Triangle Point pattern, cut triangles from the gold lamé. Appliqué triangle shapes to the neck and around the bottom of the sleeves. For the shorter triangle shapes on the sleeves, just use the triangle point.

7. Appliqué trim to the seam line of the satin and the brocade.

8. Sew front and back together at the shoulder seams.

9. Sew sleeves to coat. Sew up side seams, starting half way up the seam.

10. Placing right sides together, sew the lining.

11. Pin the lining to the coat, wrong sides together.

12. Cut the lamé into 1"-wide binding strips. Sew binding around the neck, sleeve openings, and down both sides of the front opening. Sew to the sleeve shoulder seams to finish edge.

13. Cut 3"-wide strips of fabric for the sleeve edges and the coat bottom. Sew right sides together to edges and turn to the wrong side and sew.

14. Finish the slits at the sides by folding seam allowances in and hand-stitching closed.

15. Finish star at yoke with beads, gold cord, and rhinestones. Add sequins to the coat and hang the dove from the yoke trim. See photo at right.

16. Add a gold needle at the front binding and place a feather close by.

Making the moon

1. Using the Moon pattern from page 31, cut out front and back from brocade.

2. Place angel transfer in the center of the moon front and sew around edges, followed by a frame of ribbon.

Angel transfer

3. Sew selected charms onto the moon.

4. Right sides together, sew moon front to back, leaving a 3" opening.

5. Clip excess seam allowance and turn.

6. Stuff polyester stuffing firmly into tips of moon first, then into center.

7. Hand-stitch opening closed.

8. Sew loop of ribbon to the top back point of the moon for hanging.

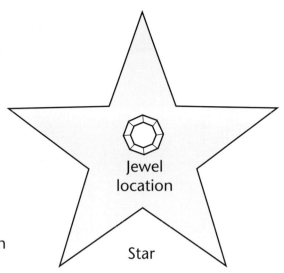

Jewel location

Star

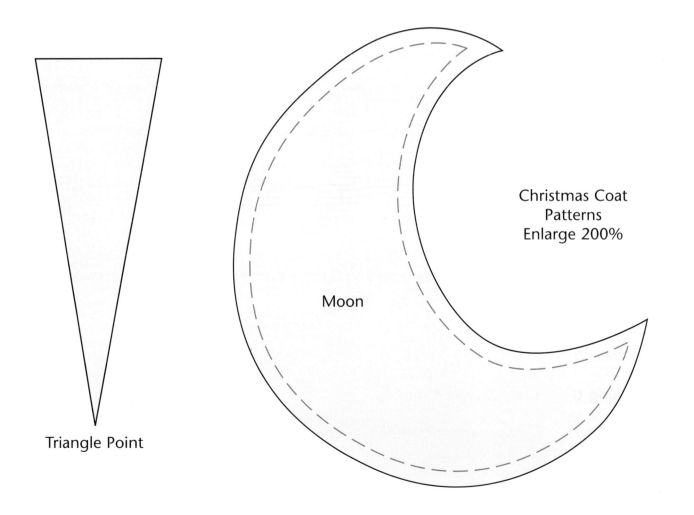

Triangle Point

Moon

Christmas Coat
Patterns
Enlarge 200%

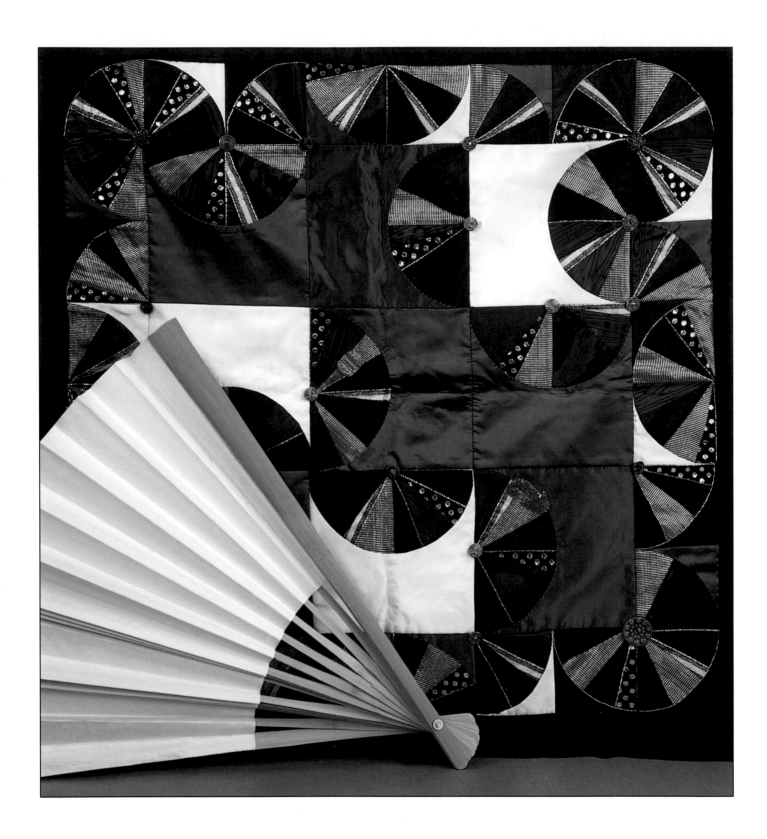

Black Quilt

Supplies:

2–4 small buckles

21 unique buttons of various sizes

Assorted strips of fabrics and ribbons for appliqué material

Black faille: 1 yd.

Black satin: ⅛ yd.

Cream faille: ¼ yd.

Flannel: 1 yd.

Muslin: 1 yd.

Olive taffeta: ⅜ yd.

Scraps of beaded trims

Threads: black, metallic gold

Note: Finished quilt size is 27½" sq.

With only three pattern pieces and no quilting at all, this richly textured fan design is as timesaving as it is sophisticated. This is a very rewarding piece to put together.

Instructions:

1. Cut a 27" square from flannel and a 31½" square from black faille.

2. Cut forty-six 3½" squares from muslin. Cut appliqué fabric and ribbons into one hundred eighty-five 4"-long strips in widths ranging from 1" to 4".

3. Using Pattern A on page 36, cut out three pieces in cream faille and six pieces in olive taffeta.

4. Using Pattern B on page 35, cut out seven pieces in cream faille, eight pieces in olive taffeta, four pieces in black faille, and eight pieces in black satin.

   Note: All seam allowances are ¼".

5. To piece the fan blocks, take a 3½" muslin square and using Pattern C from page 36, place fan shape on square as shown in Figure 1. Mark the curved top edge of the fan and the turning dot at the base onto the muslin. Repeat this step for all muslin squares.

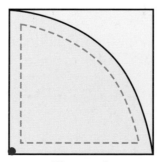

Figure 1

Note: These marks are used to place the strips of appliqué material to make the design. There should be 3–5 strips applied for each fan.

6. Place the first fabric or ribbon strip on a muslin square as shown in Figure 2, matching one long edge of the strip with the left edge of the fan. Pin to secure.

7. Fold under ¼" seam allowance on the left edge of a second strip and overlap the first strip with the second as shown in Figure 3.

   Notes: The left edge of the second strip intersects the dot marked at the base of the fan and touches the right edge of the first strip on the curved line at the top.

   If you are using ribbon instead of fabric, there is no need to turn under a seam allowance on slip-stitched edges.

8. Slip-stitch left edge of second strip to first strip. To reduce bulk, trim excess material from first strip before applying the third strip.

9. Continue to add strips as needed to cover the fan, making certain that all strips intersect at the dot and completely cover the curved line at the top of fan. See Figure 4. When all strips have been appliquéd, place Pattern C over the appliqués on the muslin square. Mark and trim along the cutting line. See Figure 5.

10. When all fans have been completed, piece quilt top together by first making the nine center blocks. Join two fan pieces together to make a half circle. Fold under seam allowance on the curved edge of one A piece, clipping the seam allowance at regular intervals to smooth the curve. Slip-stitch the A piece to the half-circle unit. See Figure 6 on page 35. Repeat to make eight more large fan blocks.

11. To piece small blocks for the border, match B pieces to the remaining single fan blocks. Once again, fold under seam allowance on curved edge of each B piece, clip seam allowances, and slip-stitch the B pieces to the curved part of the fans. This makes twenty-eight small fan blocks.

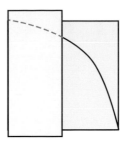

Figure 2

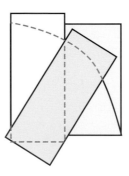

Figure 3

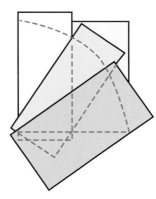

Figure 4

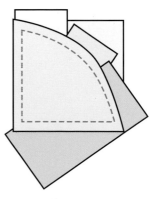

Figure 5

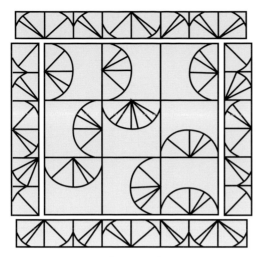

Figure 6

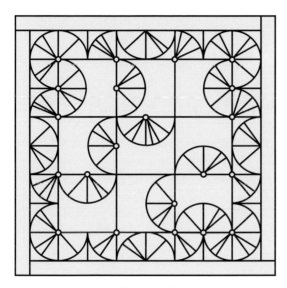

Figure 7

Pattern B

12. Join the large fan blocks to make three rows of three blocks each. See Figure 6 as a pattern to assemble the center section. See Figure 6 again to assemble the small fan blocks to form the edges of the quilt. Where black fabric or ribbon meets black, use black thread to couch gold thread onto seam lines to accent the fan shapes.

13. To add the backing and the binding, find and mark the center of the top, flannel, and back/binding piece by folding each piece into quarters. Layer the back/binding piece right side down and the top and flannel pieces right side up with the centers matched, keeping the edges parallel. Baste through all the layers to secure.

14. Fold 2" of back/binding piece to front of quilt top as shown in Figure 7, overlapping top edge of quilt. Fold under raw edge of backing ¼" for a 1¾"-wide self-binding. Slip-stitch binding to quilt top.

    Note: To keep the binding smooth, begin in the center of each strip and work out to the edges.

15. To finish, stitch on buttons as shown in Figure 7, stitching through all the layers. Stitch on buckles and scraps of beading as desired for additional embellishment.

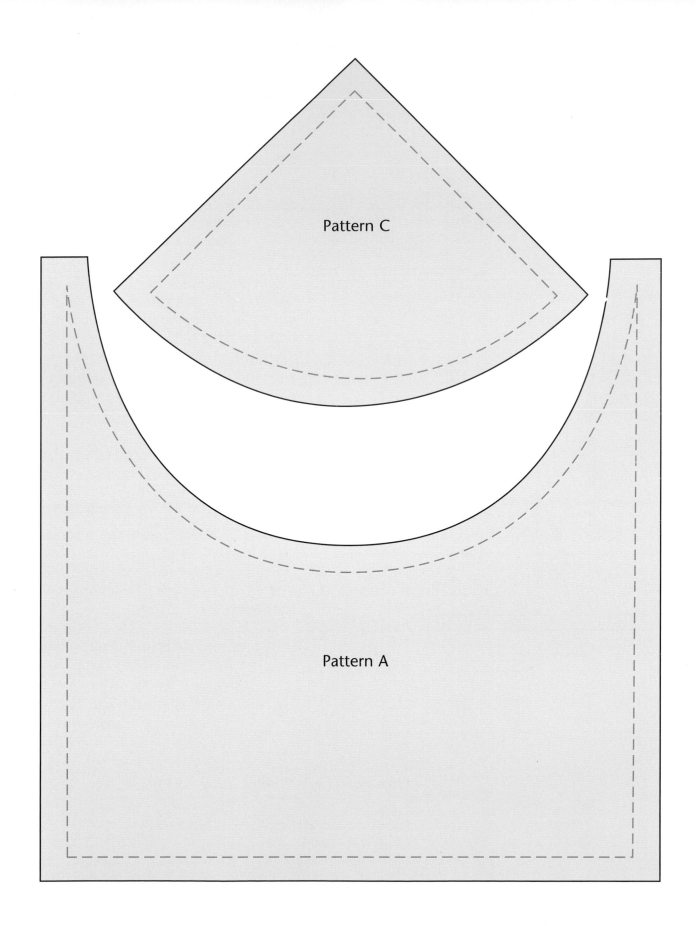

Pattern C

Pattern A

Moroccan Vest

Supplies:

Muslin: 3 yds. (Pre-shrink by wetting, then dry in medium-temperature dryer.)

One skein white perle cotton thread

Silver sequins: ½"

Thin quilt batting: 1 yd. (For a thicker textured vest, cut up a mattress pad.)

Vanishing marker

Vest pattern

Note: It is easier to work with the muslin used for the fringe if it has not been shrunk.

Tip: For a different look, use yarn instead of fabric for the fringe.

I fell in love with a large woven cape that I was told came from the mountains of Morocco. Rows of cream-colored fringe overlayed a woven base material and alternated with rows of metallic spangles. Of course, I wanted to recreate this design. I considered knitting or crocheting a similar pattern, and actually made a throw for my couch. Then I wondered about making something in fabric. A jacket would be great, but a vest would be faster.

Instructions:

1. Cut out two vest backs and four fronts from muslin.

2. Fold down seam allowances on pattern pieces and cut two fronts and one back from batting.

3. Sandwich batting between two coordinating muslin pieces and pin in place at center, near shoulders, near underarms, and along bottom.

4. Placing right sides together, sew fronts to backs at shoulder seams, trim seam allowances to ¼", press open. Cut a 1½" x 8" strip from muslin. Cut in half. Press 4" edges under ¼" and center strip over open shoulder seams, then sew it down through all layers and along both edges.

5. Lay vest right side up and mark lines for sewing fringe approximately 2½" apart either vertically or horizontally.

6. Tear strips of muslin 2½" wide by width of fabric. Layer two together, fold lengthwise and press.

   Note: The pressed line will help guide your seam along the marked line.

(Continued on page 39)

(Continued from page 37)

7. Open and center fold along marked lines, then sew down. Trim off extra length and repeat for next line. See Figure 1.

8. To create fringe, make ¼"-deep cuts along one layer of one strip, about ½" apart, then tear to stitching line. Alternate spacing of cuts on second layer of fabric and on opposite side of strips. Tear to stitching line. See Figure 2.

9. After tearing all the fringe, spray lightly with water and dry in dryer for 20 minutes.

10. With right sides together, sew up side seams, press flat, and cover with strips as in Step 4 on page 37.

11. Either bind the bottom edge or press all bottom seam allowances to the inside, then hand- or machine-stitch bottom edge closed.

12. With vanishing marker, mark a line between two rows of fringe.

13. Using perle thread, insert the needle into the lining about 2" from the top of the sequin row and bring the needle up leaving a tail in between the fabric and the batting. Knot the thread, slip a sequin on the thread, and take a tiny stitch in the same place, leaving about ½" slack so the sequin is loose. See Figure 3.

14. Sew a running stitch or chain stitch for about 2" along sequin row and then add another sequin. Repeat to the bottom of the vest. Do several rows of sequins between rows of fringe.

Notes: The sequins will withstand a washing if the vest is washed in cold water and hung to dry.

Some people choose to place the sequins closer together.

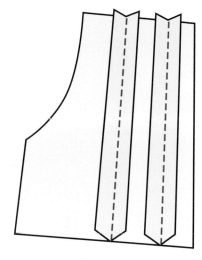

Figure 1

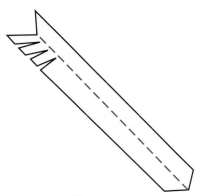

Figure 2

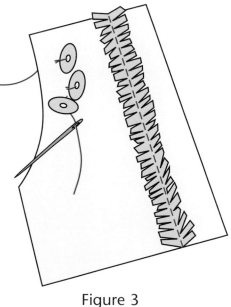

Figure 3

Vogue (vog) Scrappliqué — having a feeling that is contemporary and modern or something that feels comfortable in today's world. Stylish and fashionable with socially acceptable taste.

Vogue Scrappliqué

Patchwork Quilt

Supplies:

Assorted beads and small buttons

Brown fabric: ⅛ yd.

Green/black print fabric: ½ yd.

Pink fabric: ¼ yd.

Scraps of flannels, laces, and trims

Scraps of three assorted print fabrics

Tip: Miniature quilt projects such as this are perfect to take when traveling. Simply precut your fabric and put each square, material, and trims in a separate plastic bag.

Tip: This pattern could be used at a bridal or baby shower. Have each guest make a square, sign their name, and quilt it together for the bride or mother-to-be.

A person who enjoys quilts cannot help but want a patchwork quilt, but they take so much work to make. My solution is to make a beautiful mini quilt!

Instructions:

1. Cut pink fabric into twelve 2½" squares, sixteen 1" x 2½" sashing pieces, and five 1" x 8½" sashing pieces.

2. Use Patterns A–D on page 44. From print scrap fabric one, cut six pieces of Pattern A. From print scrap fabric two, cut six pieces of Pattern B. From print scrap fabric three, cut twelve pieces of Pattern D.

3. From brown fabric, cut twelve pieces of Pattern B, two 1" x 9" border strips, and two 1" x 11" border strips.

4. From green/black print, cut twelve pieces of Pattern C and one 15" x 18" backing piece.

5. Cut one 11" x 13½" from flannel piece.

6. Mark the twelve 2½" pink squares with ¼" seam allowances along all edges. Using Patterns A, B, C, and D minus their ¼" seam allowances, mark all twelve squares. See Figure 1.

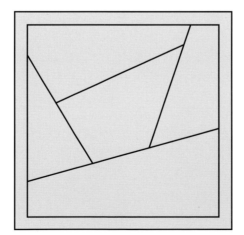

Figure 1

43

7. Place one piece of print A at top of a pink block. Fold under seam allowance on lower edge; slip-stitch. Repeat with prints B, C, and D, folding under edges that are toward center. Repeat to make all twelve blocks. Add small pieces of lace or trim as desired, securing them in seam allowances.

8. Arrange blocks in four rows of three each. Stitch blocks into rows with short sashing pieces between them. See Figure 2. Stitch rows together using long sashing pieces.

9. Stitch one 11" brown border piece to each side edge of block. Next, stitch one 9" brown border piece to the top and bottom edges. See Figure 3 on page 45.

10. Attach trims, beads, and buttons as desired. See photo on page 43 and Detail of quilt design on page 45 as references.

11. Place the backing piece wrong side up. Center the flannel and quilt top on top of backing. Baste all layers together.

12. Trim backing to 1¼" outside flannel on all edges. Fold to the front, turning under ¼" on edge to make a 1"-wide border, mitering the corners. Slip-stitch around edges.

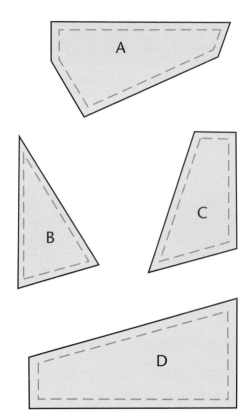

Patterns A–D
Actual Size

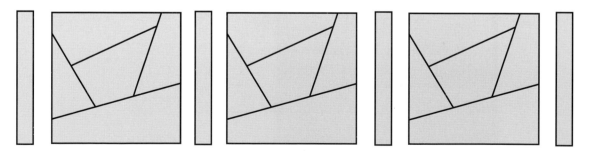

Figure 2

Figure 3
Detail of quilt design

Fanfare

Supplies:

11 rectangular buttons: ½"

21 decorative buttons: ¼"

225 copper beads

Cream linen: ¼ yd.

Cream taffeta with satin pattern: ⅝ yd.

Dark mauve moire taffeta: ¼ yd.

Dark mauve picot satin ribbon: ½" x 2½ yds.

Fleece: ⅝ yd.

Muslin: ⅝ yd.

Olive grosgrain ribbon with dot pattern: ⅝" x 1¼ yd.

Olive quilting thread

Sage green moire taffeta: ⅝ yd.

Scraps of mauve linen and olive green linen

Variegated mauve silk ribbon with gold edge: ⅝" x 1 yd.

This quilted accent pillow is especially designed to bring out the rich colors and interesting textures in an elegant room. You may choose to substitute some of the materials and/or colors to reflect the theme you have developed for your home.

Instructions:

1. Cut the cream taffeta, muslin, and fleece into 22" x 17½" pieces for the front background panel, back panel, and batting respectively.

2. Cut the cream linen into a 13½" x 6½" piece. Cut the dark mauve taffeta into a 7" x 16" piece. From the sage taffeta, cut a 13½" x 3½" piece and a 13½" x 5½" piece. These will be the main panels appliquéd onto the cream taffeta front background panel. See Figure 1.

(Continued on page 48)

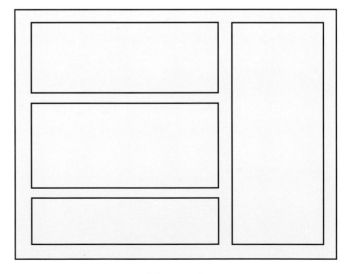

Figure 1

(Continued from page 46)

3. Cut a 2½" x 2⅓ yd. bias strip from the sage taffeta for a binding.

4. Mark placement for four panels on cream taffeta background panel.

   Note: Before marking fabrics, test to be certain marks can be removed. A hard-lead pencil may be the best choice.

5. Cut two 13½" lengths from variegated ribbon. Pin gold edge of one length in vertical center of sage 13½" x 3½" panel. Pin plain edge of second length ¼" in from right edge of sage panel.

6. Fold under seam allowances on all edges of sage panel and pin to cream taffeta background, securing ends of ribbon. Slip-stitch sage panel to cream taffeta background. Be certain to stitch ribbons in place when slip-stitching sage panel.

7. For remaining panels, fold under seam allowances on all edges and slip-stich into place as indicated in Figure 1 on page 46.

8. Using Fan Patterns on page 49, cut out two pieces each from mauve and olive linens. Fold under seam allowances.

9. Place the right angle of one olive fan ½" from the left and bottom edges of the cream linen panel and appliqué. Place the second olive fan ½" from the left and 7" from the bottom edge of the cream linen panel and appliqué.

10. Appliqué mauve linen fans ¼" inside and parallel to olive fans.

11. On dark mauve bottom panel, mark horizontal placement for three ribbons 1¼" apart with the first mark 1½" from the bottom edge. Mark vertical placement for seven ribbons 2" apart and starting 1½" from the left edge.

12. Cut three 16" lengths from dark mauve picot satin ribbon and slip-stitch on horizontal marks on the dark mauve panel. Cut seven 6½" lengths from olive grosgrain ribbon and slip-stich onto vertical marks on dark mauve panel.

13. To embellish panels, mark the left sage panel for placement of thirteen pairs of beads ½" apart at 1" intervals, beginning ½" from top edge. Stitch one bead onto each mark.

14. On the mauve fans, mark placement for beads on a ½" grid, beginning ¼" from both the left and bottom straight edges of mauve fan. Also mark placement for one bead ½" from point of scallop on olive fan. Stitch one bead on each mark.

15. Cut two 18" lengths from dark mauve picot satin ribbon. Fold into 3"-wide bows. Tack to lower-left corner of each mauve fan. Stitch one ½" decorative button at center of each bow.

16. For right sage panel, mark placement for three columns of thirteen pairs of beads ½" from top edge. Stitch one bead onto each mark, omitting the center pair of beads on the center column. Mark placement for buttons, beginning with the center column with one between the third and fourth pairs of beads, one in the center, and one between the ninth and tenth pairs of beads. Next, mark button placement between columns of beads about 3½" apart, beginning 1" from top edge. Stitch one rectangular button to each mark.

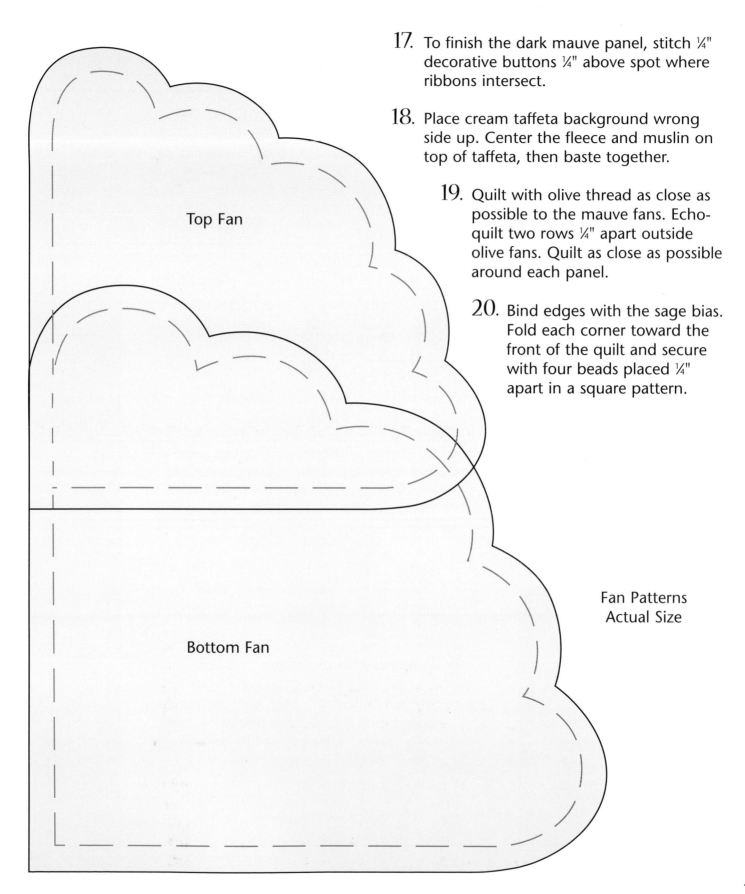

17. To finish the dark mauve panel, stitch ¼"
decorative buttons ¼" above spot where
ribbons intersect.

18. Place cream taffeta background wrong
side up. Center the fleece and muslin on
top of taffeta, then baste together.

19. Quilt with olive thread as close as
possible to the mauve fans. Echo-
quilt two rows ¼" apart outside
olive fans. Quilt as close as possible
around each panel.

20. Bind edges with the sage bias.
Fold each corner toward the
front of the quilt and secure
with four beads placed ¼"
apart in a square pattern.

Top Fan

Bottom Fan

Fan Patterns
Actual Size

49

Chinese Dragon

Designed by Shauna Kawasaki

Supplies:

Batting: about ½ yd.

Beads of various sizes

Black cord

Denim jacket with few seams

Four colors of cotton fabrics (A, B, C, D): in small prints in dusty shades, about ⅓ yd. each

Perle cotton threads: #5 or #8, various colors

Six or more small tassels

Detail of dragon tail

Shauna happened onto a denim jacket styled like a Chinese robe that closed in the center with frogs, and it seemed to her that a dragon belonged across the back.

Instructions:

1. Measure jacket width from sleeve tip to sleeve tip.

2. Copy Dragon Patterns on pages 52–54 and play with the pieces until you are pleased with the arrangement. This jacket has the head on the left shoulder. One outstretched dragon forearm goes along the left sleeve and the other forearm and shoulder are arranged to look bent across the upper body. One back leg goes down the right side of the jacket. The tail goes along the right sleeve, wrapping around it.

3. Choose fabric that coordinates with the denim, such as dusty shades of blue, green, pink, and purple, all with small print designs.

4. Select pattern pieces one at a time to cut out from fabrics and pin in place on the jacket. Cut the body and tail pieces from fabric A and cut a piece of batting to go under A that is slightly smaller.

5. Pin body in place, making certain the tail wraps around the right sleeve.

6. The head and beard are cut from fabric B along with batting slightly smaller. Pin in place.

7. Cut forelegs and shoulder, back leg and thigh, tongue, and nostrils from fabric C, then pin in place.

8. Cut eyes and flame piece for mouth from fabric D.

9. Using al four prints, cut 2" triangles for spines along his shoulders, legs, and along his back. These are not padded. Pin in place, some overlapping to emphasize the legs and arms.

10. Using perle cotton thread colors randomly, alternate buttonhole stitch, feather stitch, and running stitch along the raw edges of fabric pieces. Attach a bead every here-and-there to add glitz, glamour, and texture.

    Note: Some parts of the dragon are only stitched on the edges, but those with batting should be stitched through the center areas and randomly beaded to quilt them.

11. Small tassels are added to the knees, horns, and elbows of the dragon and black cord is couched down from the nostrils for a barbel.

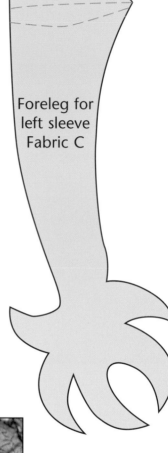

Dragon Patterns
Enlarge 300%

Body & beard here

Foreleg for
left sleeve
Fabric C

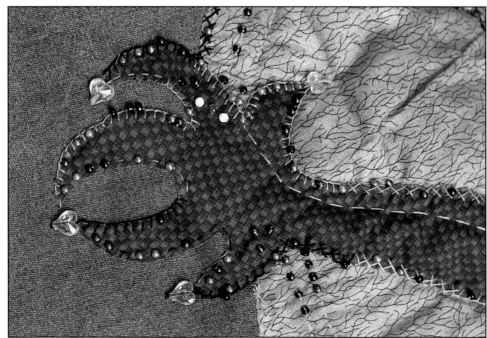

Details of stitching and beading on dragon foot

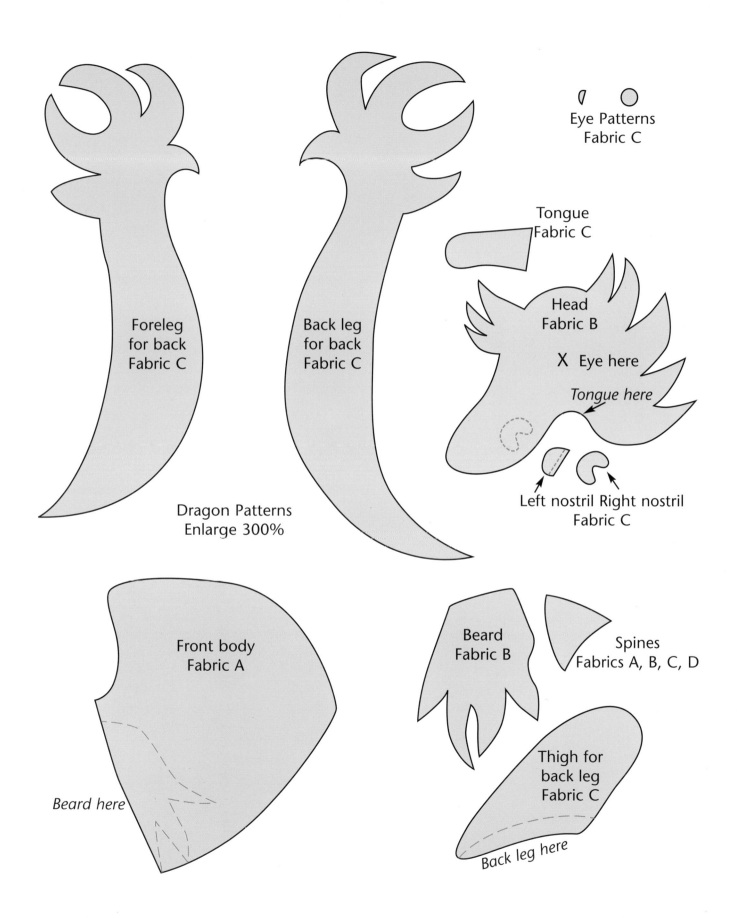

Foreleg
for back
Fabric C

Back leg
for back
Fabric C

Eye Patterns
Fabric C

Tongue
Fabric C

Head
Fabric B

X Eye here

Tongue here

Left nostril Right nostril
Fabric C

Dragon Patterns
Enlarge 300%

Front body
Fabric A

Beard here

Beard
Fabric B

Spines
Fabrics A, B, C, D

Thigh for
back leg
Fabric C

Back leg here

53

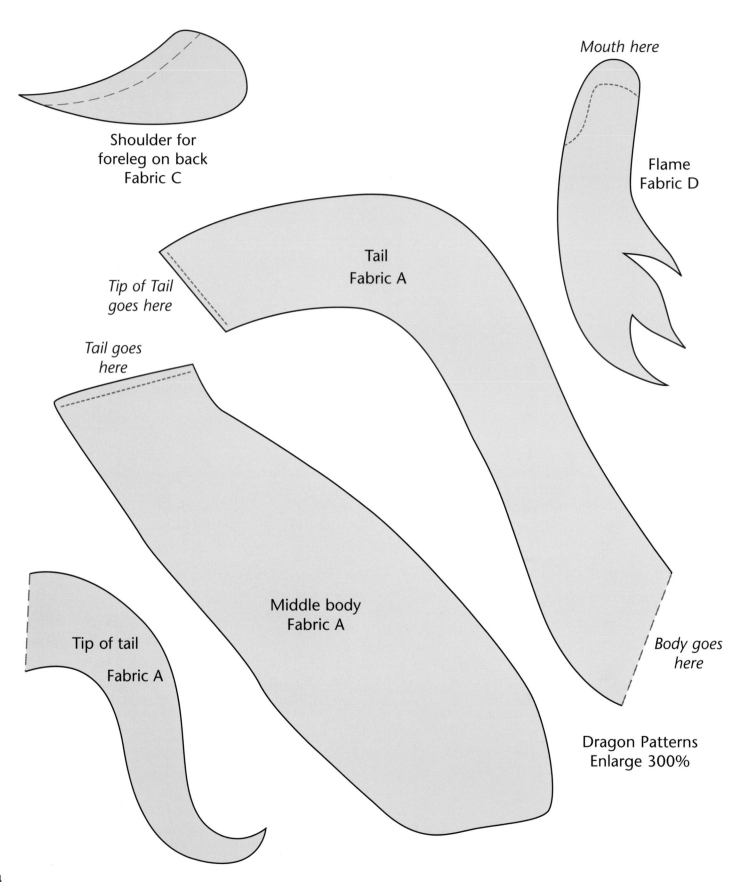

Shoulder for
foreleg on back
Fabric C

Mouth here

Flame
Fabric D

Tail
Fabric A

Tip of Tail
goes here

Tail goes
here

Middle body
Fabric A

Body goes
here

Tip of tail

Fabric A

Dragon Patterns
Enlarge 300%

Details of appliqué work on dragon face and beard

Stitching and beading detail on jacket sleeve

55

Jade Squares

Supplies:

Beads and charms (optional)

Chenille needle

Fabric for outer surface of squares: 30" x 45"

Fabric: gold lamé for lining, 30" x 45"

Gold crochet thread or perle cotton thread

Rubber stamp and gold embossing powder

Very thin batting: 1 yd.

When I visited the exhibit of art treasures from the Imperial Tombs of China, I was transfixed by the jade burial suit made of hundreds of 2" squares of jade, drilled in each corner and joined by gold wire to cover the royal person from head to toe. I wondered if this technique of joining squares of jade with wire could be translated into fabric? I went home and began cutting out and sewing up squares and immediately decided that 2" was going to be too small, so I switched to a larger square. I went back several times to look at the gold wire, and the connecting knot and came up with my version of a jade vest—not for burial, but for a festive occasion.

Instructions:

1. Cut thirty-six 4" squares for outer surface. Cut thirty-six 4" squares for linings. Cut the batting into thirty-six 3½" squares. Quarter six of them if desired.

2. Appliqué, rubber stamp, or embroider some of the outer surface squares. Plan arrangement.

3. Stack the three layers together: top fabric and lining right sides together, and batting behind the lining. Sew three sides, using ¼" seam allowance. Clip the corners, trim batting, turn, and using point turner, push corners fully out. Tuck in the ¼" seam allowance at the opening and blind-stitch it shut.

Tip: The connected squares could be done in country prints connected by yarn or very narrow ribbon; African prints connected by raffia or hemp string; dyed and appliquéd muslin, embossed velvet, batiks, brocades and many other combinations.

Detail on embellishments

4. Lay out the squares to form the two fronts and the back. See Figure 1.

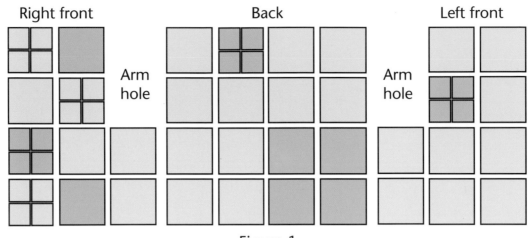

Figure 1

5. With a sharp needle that has a large enough eye for the gold thread (or yarn, perle cotton, or whatever you choose), follow Making the Knot below and on page 59 for joining the squares.

6. Add beads and charms as embellishment.

Making the Knot

1. Where four squares meet, imagine points A, B, C, and D are just ⅛" in from the corners of the squares. See Steps 1–3 in Figure 2.

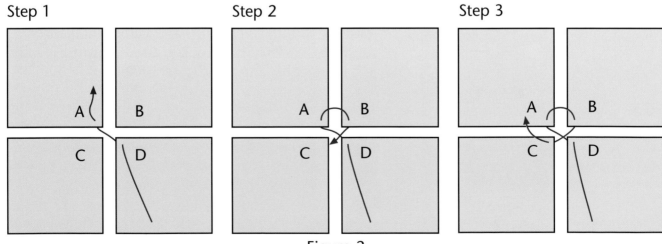

Figure 2

2. Push needle down through D corner, leaving a 3" tail. Come up at A.

3. Holding the tail in place with your left hand, push needle down at corner B. Come up at corner C.

4. Adjust tension of threads until the four corners meet. Insert needle into space between A and B (not into any fabric). Take needle under the center of the X formed by the crossed threads. Bring up into space between C and D. Pull snug.

5. Cut thread from needle about 3" from X. Tie the tails together, right over left and left over right, for a square knot. Place a dab of white glue on the knot. Leave the 3" tails or trim no closer than ½" from the knot. See Figure 3.

6. When joining only two squares, go down at corner B, leaving a 3" tail. Come up at corner A. See Figure 4.

7. Lay tail across from B to A behind where thread comes out at B. Pull to bring squares together.

8. Holding tail in place with left hand, push needle down in space above thread between the two squares.

9. Come up below the thread. Clip thread from needle 3" from fabric. Tie the tails together in a square knot. Trim as before.

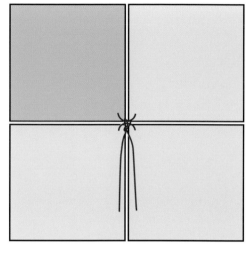

Figure 3

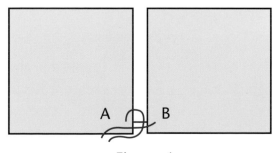

Figure 4

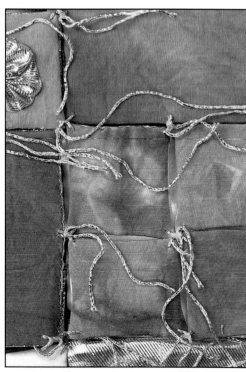

Detail on squares and knots

Scented Card

Supplies:

3–4 tablespoons dried lavender (May be found at some health food stores.)

Craft glue

Paper for inside of card: plain or patterned

Purchased blank cards and envelopes (Or cut your own from card stock.)

Scrap of ribbon or trim

Scraps of organza and gossamer wire-edged ribbons

Note: Use old sewing-machine needles to sew into paper because it will ruin a good needle.

Tip: A charm, bead, or button may be added to the card to make it more personal.

When you need a simple, thoughtful greeting card for a special occasion or a gift—put together a sachet card quickly and easily.

Instructions:

1. Cut a piece of organza 1" smaller than card front. Sew scrap of ribbon or fabric to center. Using an old needle, set your machine on the longest stitch and sew two sides and bottom edge of organza, allowing a little slack so there will be room for the lavender. A straight stitch or zigzag stitch works here. Add 3–4 tablespoons of dried lavender. See Figure 1. Sew top edge closed.

Figure 1

2. Leave card as is, or zigzag stitch ribbon along edges. Cut ribbon ends at a slant to create mitered corners.

3. Cut a piece of paper just ¼" smaller than dimensions of open card. Fold in half and crease. Glue to the inside of the card to cover the stitching lines.

Old Cat

Supplies:

Cardboard or soft plastic

Craft knife

Embroidery flosses:
gray, dark green, pink

Embroidery needle

Fat quarter of gray wool

Gray sport-weight yarn

Polyester stuffing

Scrap of white felt, 3" sq.

Very small scraps of
colored wool or felts

Tip: The pattern can be reduced by half to create "3 little kittens" and their mittens, perhaps of felt. To keep the mittens from getting lost, tie a piece of yarn to them that passes across the back and catch-stitch to the nape of the neck.

It may not be chic or elegant, but this scruffy old cat is nice to have around. People can play with him without "ruining" him. He was made scruffy and he stays scruffy.

Instructions:

1. Enlarge and cut out Old Cat Patterns on pages 64–65.

2. Cut out cat body from gray wool. Cut one 3" x 12" piece for tail. Cut one oval from cardboard.

3. Cut oval of white felt for face. Embroider around eyes with a chain stitch and pupils with a long stitch. Lay a 3" piece of gray yarn across face and embroider a tiny pink triangle for the nose in the center. Unravel the strands of the yarn to create whiskers. Cut two tiny slivers of gray felt for eyelids and tack on over upper eyes.

4. Cut gray yarn into thirty 4½"-long pieces. Lay them side by side, (making a beard about 2" wide), and sew across top edges by machine. Pin in place under lower half of white felt circle face and satin-stitch face and beard in place. Unravel every third or fourth piece of yarn.

5. Using colored wool or felt scraps in subdued colors, cut four or five patches for front and back of cat. Sew in place by machine.

6. Sew feet, wrong sides together. Leave top of feet open. Fray edges and stuff with polyester stuffing. Pin to center-bottom edge of front body piece.

7. Sew the paws, wrong sides together. Leave top of paw open. Fray edges and stuff.

8. Place the front and back of the body wrong sides together. Slip the top of the arms about ½" in between the front and back at the mark on each side. Sew around the cat body, being certain to catch the arms securely in the seam. Leave the bottom open. Fray edges and stuff.

9. Sandwich cardboard or plastic oval between the two wool oval pieces. Sew around edges, wrong sides together, using ¼" seam allowance. Fray edges.

10. Sew oval into opening at the bottom of the cat. This helps the cat to sit on a flat surface.

11. Fold tail piece, wrong sides together. Sew long edge and fray. Hand-stitch to back of cat.

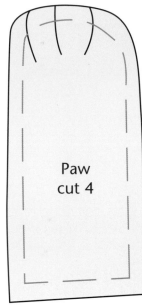

Paw
cut 4

Old Cat
Patterns
Enlarge 150%

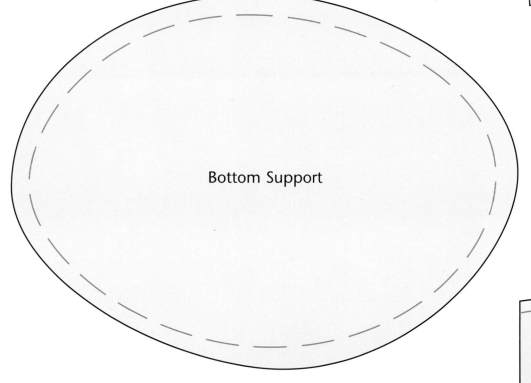

Bottom Support

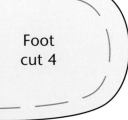

Foot
cut 4

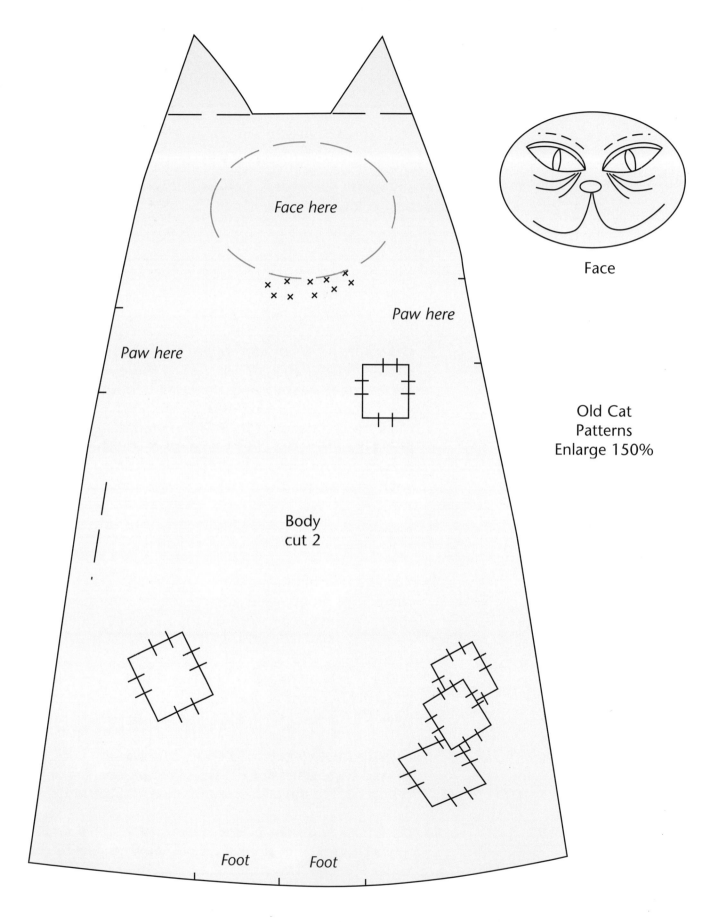

Face here

x x x x x
x x x

Paw here

Paw here

Body
cut 2

Foot   Foot

Face

Old Cat
Patterns
Enlarge 150%

Rag Pillow

Supplies:

Black twill for back: ½ yd. (Or whatever you prefer in cotton or corduroy.)

Disappearing marker

Muslin: 13" sq. (Prewash all muslin.)

Muslin for strips: ¼–⅓ yd.

Pillow form: 18" sq.

Optional Fringe Pillow

This variation uses yarn instead of torn strips of fabric. Cut 5" lengths from yarn. Stitch a group of three pieces of yarn across the middle, using a zigzag stitch at the markings.

Pillows are some of the best and easiest accents to place in any room. Sometimes, however, it is hard to find the perfect pillow—so make it!

Instructions:

1. Tear ¼ yd. piece of muslin into strips 1" x 9", then tear each 9" length in half for "rags."

2. Draw lines across muslin square inside ½" seam allowances and about 2" apart. You may wish to stagger the rows. Make marks along lines about 1½" apart.

3. Mark lines on muslin square with disappearing marker inside the seam allowance about every 2". Then make marks on the rows about 1½" apart. You may wish to stagger the marks on alternating rows.

4. Cut two 4" x 13" pieces and two 4" x 19" pieces from black fabric for border.

5. Keeping rags out of the way of the seams, sew the two short strips on opposite sides of the muslin square then sew the longer strips on the remaining sides.

6. Cut two 12" x 19" back pieces. Press one long edge under ½", then press a 1½" hem and sew. If you plan to close the back with buttons, do buttonholes and buttons. Or stitch on large snaps, Velcro, or ties.

7. Overlap the two hemmed edges to make the back 19" sq. and baste-stitch at each side. Use this opening at the center back of the pillowcase for inserting the form.

8. Place back and front pieces right sides together and sew all edges. Turn right sides out. Insert pillow form.

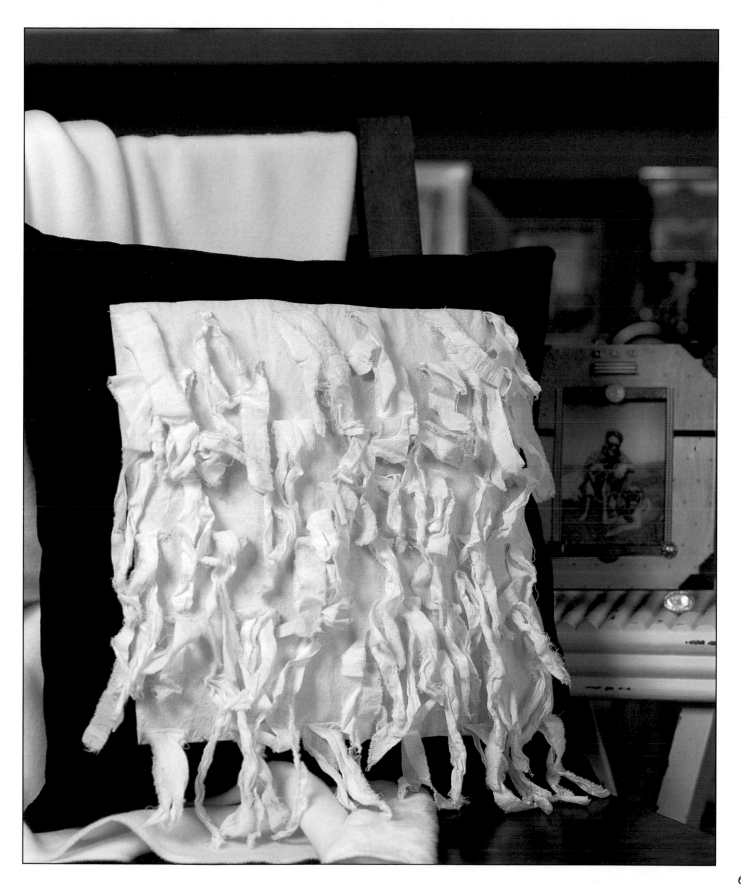

Leather Rug

Supplies:

Heavy-duty upholstery thread

Leather-point needle for sewing machine

Paint or dye to color burlap or canvas backing (optional)

Rug-hooking burlap or canvas: 4' x 6'

Scissors to cut leather

Several pounds of soft leather scraps: colored or natural tanned

Note: To clean a leather rug, take outside and with a partner shake the rug vigorously to remove dirt and particles. The rug can also be hung and beaten, but only from the back side, or the loose ends will break off.

This is truly a unique and beautiful rug. Because it is made of suede, it feels wonderful when you walk on it in bare feet and it adds an interesting texture in any room.

Instructions:

Sewing Method I

1. Sort through the leather scraps. Pull out all pieces that are ½"–¾" wide and 6"–12" in length and set aside. Cut the remaining leather to the above measurements. Do not make them all the same. You want a large variety.

2. Replace the needle in your sewing machine with the leather-point needle and thread with upholstery thread. Beginning in the center of the rug, lay strips across the short length of the backing. Sew down the center of the leather strip, leaving 2"–4" of the ends hanging free. Repeat across entire width of backing.

3. Begin the next row directly next to the first row, covering as much of the backing as possible. Be certain to vary the length of the ends that are left loose and snug the next piece of leather as close to the last as possible. Continue until one half of rug is completed, then start from the middle and do the other side.

Sewing Method II

1. Sort and cut leather scraps into strips as described in Step 1 above.

2. Fold the leather strips in half and sew across the center of the strip. Start in the center of the backing and work out to the edges. Place the strips as close together as possible to allow as little as possible of the backing to show through.

Traditional (tra-di-shanal) Scrappliqué —
having a style or technique that follows a
well-established pattern. An item which is
timeless in taste and appeal.

Traditional Scrappliqué

Pillow Ornament

Supplies:

Polyester stuffing

Ribbon: ⅜" x ¼ yd.

Scraps of mauve and burgundy fabrics

Scraps of rose fabric: 4" x 8"

Two wooden beads: 8mm

Vintage embroidered piece: 2" sq.

Note: Embroidery Patterns on page 74 may be used with selected fabrics if desired.

Home-made ornaments can be the highlight of any holiday. Try these tiny scrappliquéd pillow ornaments for a delightful new addition to your next holiday.

Instructions:

1. Cut out two pillow pieces, using Pillow Ornament Patterns on page 74, from rose fabric. Cut four corner pieces from mauve and burgundy fabrics.

2. Fold ¼" seam allowance under on all edges of embroidered pieces.

3. Center and slip-stitch embroidered piece to one piece of pillow fabric.

4. Place two corner pieces with right sides together and stitch one short edge up to inside seam allowance. See Figure 1.

5. Repeat with two remaining corner pieces to make a four-corner unit.

6. Fold inside straight-edge seam allowances of corner unit under and place right sides up on top of embroidered piece. Stitch to design piece.

7. With right sides together stitch pillow front to pillow back, leaving a 1" opening for turning.

8. Sew a running stitch in the seam allowance in one corner and pull to slightly gather. Repeat for all remaining corners.

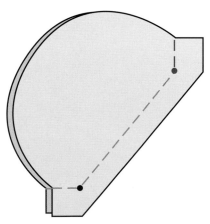

Figure 1

9. Turn and stuff ornament. Stitch opening closed.

10. Fold ribbon in half and thread ends through beads. Knot ends together and stitch to the top of ornament for a hanger.

**Embroidery Patterns
Actual Size**

Stitch Key
1 Satin stitch
2 Stem stitch

Color Key
(Note: Numbers are for DMC floss)
A 807 Peacock Blue
B 797 Royal Blue
C 954 Nile Green
D 895 Christmas Green—dk.
E 315 Antique Mauve—vy. dk.

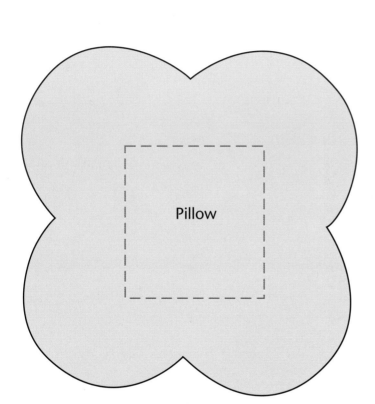

**Pillow Ornament Patterns
Actual Size**

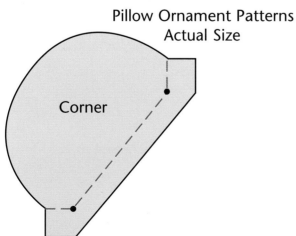

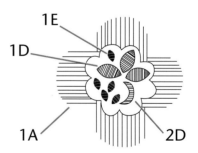

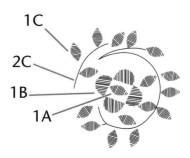

Quilted Stocking

Supplies:

Dark green print: ⅛ yd.

Eight green pebble beads: 3mm

Embroidery flosses: aqua, dark green, white

Pink bias tape: 1" x ¾ yd.

Scraps of fabrics: heavy cotton, muslin, assorted colors, prints, stripes

Scraps of fleece

Three white buttons

Tip: Small Christmas stocking ornaments can be made for each child every year. Save a favorite outfit or dress as it is outgrown. Cut up the fabric to use in making the stocking. Date each piece on the back. These tiny treasures will bring back memories for years to come.

Christmas stockings are more cherished if they are one-of-a-kind and lovingly made for your special person. This ornament-sized stocking will be treasured forever.

Instructions:

1. Make two copies of the Quilted Stocking Pattern on page 78. Use one to cut up and use for appliqué pattern pieces. Add ¼" seam allowance to all appliqué pieces before cutting fabric.

2. Using a whole stocking pattern, cut one each from heavy cotton, fleece, and muslin.

3. Cut two stocking patterns from green print fabric.

4. Cut one 2¼" x 5" piece from green print fabric.

5. From plain pink fabric, cut two ¾" x 1" pieces. From striped fabric, cut one 1" x 1¼" piece.

6. Cut out appliqué patterns from assorted fabrics, using the cut-up stocking pattern. Stitch appliqués to heavy cotton stocking piece, except for the appliqué square between the fans.

7. Stitch the pink ¾" x 1" pieces to the striped 1" x 1¼" piece on opposite sides. Trim to 1¼" sq. Stitch to cotton front on the diagonal between the fans.

8. Stack muslin, fleece, and cotton stocking pieces together with the cotton right side up. Quilt as desired. Embellish the stocking as follows: Use two strands of aqua floss. Satin-stitch a band 1" from top of stocking. Couch across the aqua band with a green print band of fabric.

9. With white floss, satin-stitch a small circle to the bottom point of each fan.

10. Satin-stitch and then backstitch both arrow points. Outline-stitch top of center piece.

11. Outline-stitch the zigzag patterns on bottom half of stocking, attach buttons and beads as indicated on pattern.

12. Fold the 2¼" x 5" piece of fabric in half lengthwise and press. Fold long edges under ¼" and press.

13. Stitch to top of stocking front.

14. Stitch two green print stocking pieces, with right sides together, along top edge. Turn and press.

15. Place stocking front right side up on green print and baste raw edges together.

16. Bind around raw edge with bias tape and form a 1½" loop hanger at the upper-right corner of the stocking. Tuck end under and stitch to back.

17. Further decorate stocking with buttons, beads, or charms.

Note: Because it is a Christmas ornament, this quilted stocking is difficult to overdecorate.

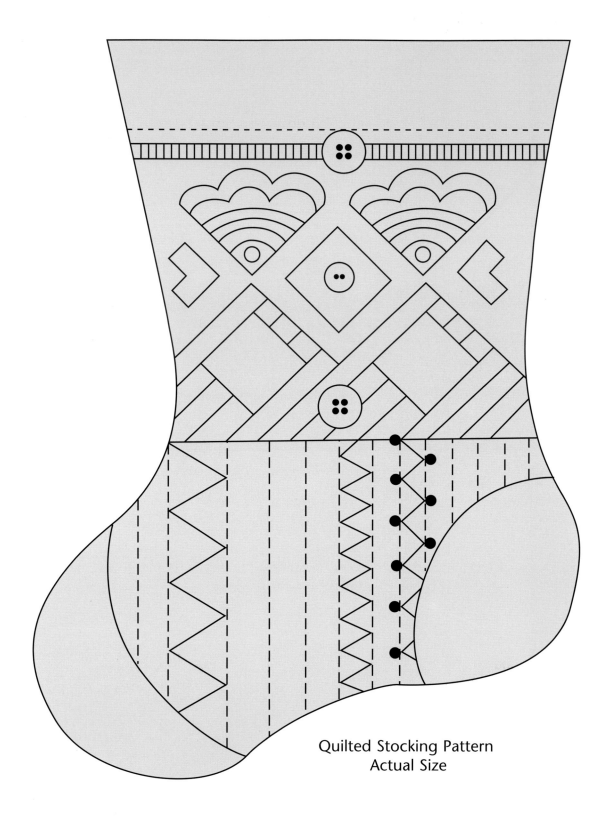

Quilted Stocking Pattern
Actual Size

Rose Quilt Block

Designed by Miriam Gourley

Supplies:

Coordinating cotton prints to surround quilt block in a modified log cabin arrangement: seven colors or as desired

Embroidery flosses or perle cotton threads: green for leaves, rose for assembling the rose

Pale green fabric for two leaves

Rose-colored cotton fabric strips: 1" x 22"

White fabric for block centers: 5½" sq.

Yarn needle

Tip: This is the perfect quilt to make at a bridal shower. Have different colored fabrics for each guest to make a rose, then have them date and sign each square with a wish for the bride.

Miriam Gourley has adapted a silk-ribbon embroidery technique to be used with narrow strips of fabric. The strip, as it is turned first to the right side then to the wrong side, creates a subtle color variation. This is really an embroidery technique; but in this case, bits of fabric scraps are used to make an interesting rose.

Instructions:

1. The square is 3" sq. The strips are 1½"–2" wide. Use ¼" seam allowances. Assemble the quilt block.

2. Using all six strands of embroidery floss in the needle, stitch a 2½"–3"-tall fly stitch in the center of the quilting block. Come up at A, go down at B, and come up at C, bringing the needle tip over the floss. See Figure 1. Go down at D, forming a catch stitch. Add a diagonal bar of equal length on each side of the Y. This will make a total of five spokes of floss. Knot floss at back of block, leaving a workable length dangling. You will use this to anchor the ends of the fabric strip when you have finished weaving the rose.

(Continued on page 81)

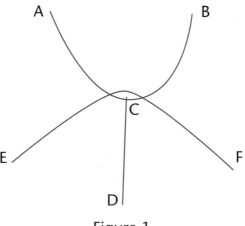

Figure 1

(Continued from page 79)

3. Thread the strip of rose fabric into a yarn needle and come up at the center of the spokes. Working in a counterclockwise direction, weave the fabric strip over and under the floss spokes beginning in the center and moving out with each round. Allow the fabric to twist but remain loose as you work. Weave until all the spokes are covered. Bring the end of the fabric strip to the back side of the quilting block and use the length of floss to tie both ends together securely. See Figure 2.

Detail of rose and leaves

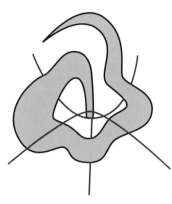

Figure 2

4. Make templates from paper, using the Leaf Pattern. Pin each template to a piece of doubled leaf fabric and stitch completely around the leaf on the pattern line.

   Note: Use old sewing-machine needles to sew into paper because it will ruin a good needle.

5. Remove the templates. Make a slit in one side of each fabric leaf and turn right side out. Press.

6. Blind-stitch the leaves in place on the quilt. Use one strand of green floss and outline-stitch down the center of each leaf. Make straight stitches for the veins.

Leaf Pattern

Tip: This quilt can also be made from satin or velvet materials for a more elegant vintage piece.

Radish Garden Quilt

Supplies:

Dark red fabric: ¼ yd.

Five pink buttons: ¼"

Fleece: ½ yd.

Green embroidery floss

Green-and-cream striped fabric: ⅛ yd.

Mauve print fabric: ¼ yd.

Muslin: 7" x 9"

Olive wide-wale corduroy: ⅜ yd.

Pink-and-white striped fabric: ¾" x 4¾"

Rose fabric: 1¼ yd.

Scraps of fabrics: burgundy, green, and dark green

Scraps of white-and-mauve print fabric

Bright, crisp radishes adorn a miniature quilt, perfect for a kitchen or breakfast nook.

Instructions:

1. Enlarge Radish Patterns on pages 84–86. Add seam allowances where appropriate.

2. From corduroy, cut two 7" x 9" pieces, one on the bias.

3. From dark green fabric, cut one each of patterns A–G.

4. From green fabric, cut one each of patterns H and I and one piece 2½" sq.

5. From green/cream-striped fabric, cut six 1¾" x 7" sashing strips and four 1¾" x 9" sashing strips.

6. From burgundy fabric, cut one each of patterns J–L.

7. From dark red fabric, cut one 7" x 9" piece, one 4¾" sq. piece, and one each of patterns M, N, and P.

8. From rose fabric, cut one 32" x 19" backing piece and cut a 1¼" x 3 yd. bias strip.

9. From mauve print fabric, cut eight of pattern Q on page 84.

10. From fleece, cut a 32" x 19" piece.

11. To make left block, transfer patterns A–N to wrong side of bias-cut corduroy piece, centering pattern in block.

12. Appliqué pieces A through N in place.

13. Center block is a reverse appliqué. See Figure 1. Mark position of radishes on muslin as indicated in Figure 2 on page 85. Trace pattern O onto muslin.

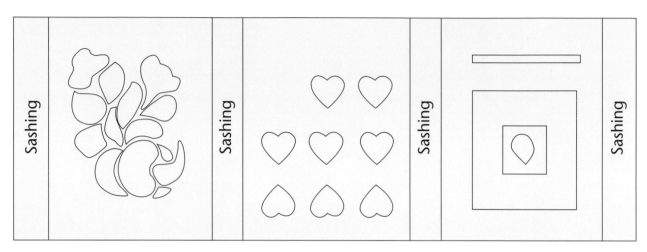

Figure 1

14. Cut out muslin ⅛" inside each radish outline. Place muslin over dark red 7" x 9" piece and align edges. Baste fabrics together.

15. Fold under edges of muslin opening to the radish outlines and slip-stitch edges with white thread.

16. Transfer radish top from pattern O to appropriate position above each radish. Using two strands of floss, satin stitch radish tops.

17. Using white thread, decorate radishes with running stitch. See pattern O. Mark three short, curved lines at the bottom of each radish for roots and stitch along lines with running stitch, using red thread.

18. To appliqué right block, fold edges of dark red 4¾" square under ¼". Topstitch to wrong side of remaining corduroy piece, 2¾" below and parallel to one short edge. Center horizontally.

19. Fold edges of green 2½" square under ¼". Center on dark red piece and appliqué in place.

Radish Pattern O
Enlarge 200%

Pattern Q
Actual Size

84

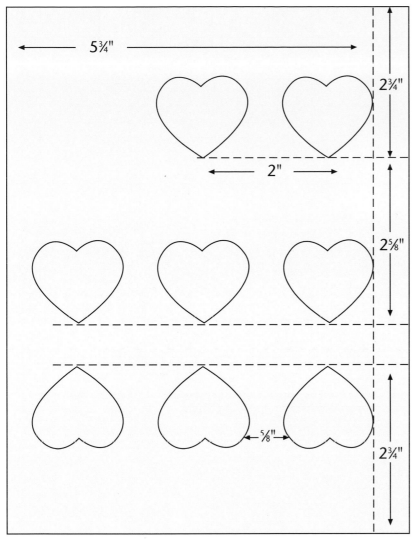

Figure 2

Radish Pattern P
Enlarge 200%

20. Fold under edges of piece P ¼" and appliqué onto center of green square. Remember when positioning radish to leave room for radish top.

21. Transfer radish top from pattern P onto green square and fill in shape with running stitch and white thread.

22. Fold edges of pink strip under ¼" and appliqué to corduroy piece 1" above dark red piece. See Figure 1 on page 84. Stitch pink buttons to pink strip, centering first button and placing remaining buttons ½" apart on either side.

23. Stitch sashing strips between squares. Finished sashing is 1¼"-wide.

24. With right sides facing, sew 3" x 27" mauve print border strips to top and bottom of pieced center.

25. Sew 3" x 17½" mauve print border strips to the sides of the piece.

26. Layer rose backing piece wrong side up, fleece, then quilt top right side up. Baste horizontally and vertically. Quilt as desired.

27. Bind edges.

Add ¼" Seam Allowances

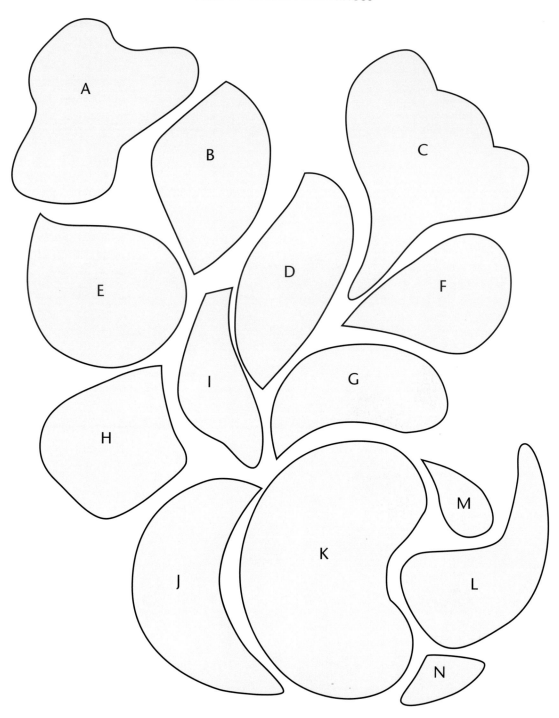

Radish Patterns A–N
Actual Size

Tin Bucket

Supplies:

Scraps of various fabrics

Tin bucket

Upholstery trim

Want to do something a bit different? Try scrappliqué on the hard surface of a tin bucket.

Instructions:

1. Cut various fabric into pieces approximately 3" sq. Fabric block edges may be hemmed or left to fray.

   Note: Larger pieces are difficult to place and smooth.

2. Using fabric glue, apply fabric squares to sides of the bucket.

3. When bucket is completely covered with fabric, glue upholstery trim to top and bottom rims.

   Tip: Embellish bucket with charms, beads, buttons, tassels, or fabric affixed with heat-transferred photographs.

   Tip: Coat fabric-covered bucket with several coats of decoupage medium so that it will be easier to wipe off.

Fan Quilt Blocks

Traditional Scrappliqué Design

Supplies:

Muslin for log cabin block: 5¾" sq.

Print fabric for fan block: 5¾" sq.

Scraps of large floral fabric for fans

Scraps of light and dark fabrics for log cabin strips

Scraps of striped fabric for fan top

Note: The materials listed are for one fan and one log cabin block.

There are forty-one fan and forty-one log cabin blocks in the pictured quilt. The log cabin blocks are assembled in three ways. Dark fabric with light, medium with light, and dark with medium.

Tip: If a fabric seems too bright, turn the fabric over. The same pattern will be shown, but with more-subdued colors.

This quilt design is popular due to its exciting visual elements. The log cabin blocks in this quilt are arranged in such a way as to create interesting diagonals.

Instructions:

Fan Block

1. Trace and cut out Fan Patterns on page 90. Cut out fan pieces. Center the Pattern A over the print to include a large flower in the fan.

2. With rights sides together stitch piece A to piece B.

3. Appliqué the fan to the 5¾" print square as shown in picture to the right.

Log Cabin Block

1. Cut or tear the light and dark fabrics for the log cabin block into strips 1¼" wide.

2. Use the stitch-and-trim method with ¼" seam allowances to make the log cabin blocks. Cut two 1¼" squares. Place the first square in the upper-left corner of the muslin square. Pin the second square to the first, with right sides together, and stitch through all layers along right-hand edge of squares. Press seam allowances toward the muslin.

3. Place a 2"-long dark strip on top of the two squares and stitch through all layers along the long edge. Trim and press seam allowance toward dark fabric. Continue to add strips, alternating light and dark and trimming to size after each seam until the block is full.

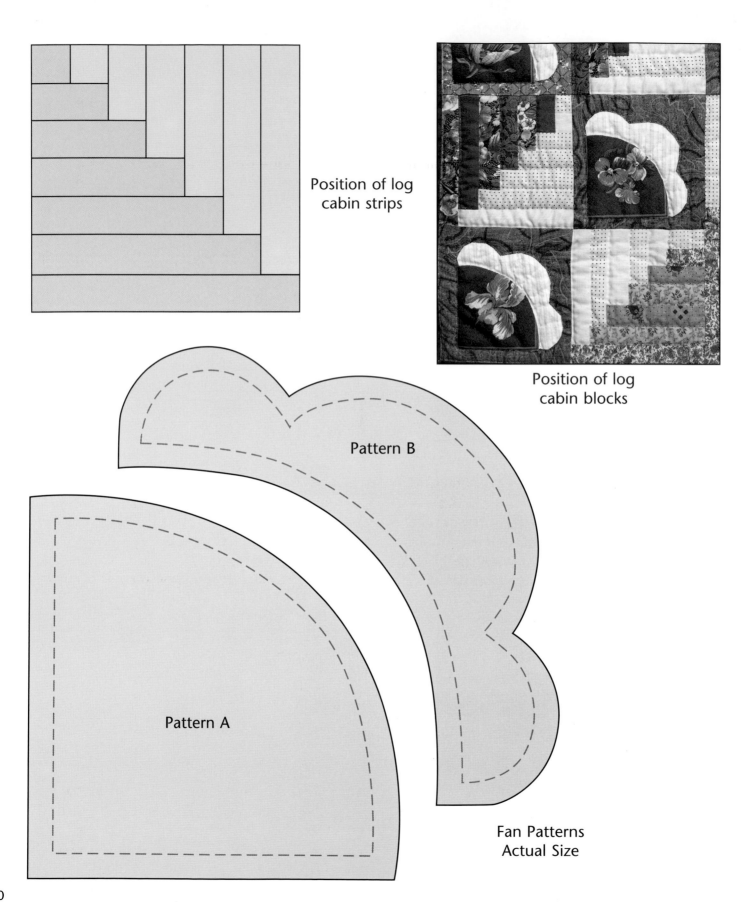

Position of log
cabin strips

Position of log
cabin blocks

Pattern B

Pattern A

Fan Patterns
Actual Size

Lady Liberty

Designed by Miriam Gourley

Supplies:

Backing fabric: ½ yard

Black quilting thread

Buttons for closing

Embroidery flosses: red, white

Pillow form: 20" sq.

Red lipstick

Scraps of different print cottons for face, hands, robe, skirt, socks, and trim

Scraps of felts: black, brown, gold, orange, white

Two black cotton fabric pieces 12" x 21" for pillow back and one 21" sq. for pillow front

Note: Use old sewing-machine needles to sew into paper because it will ruin a good needle.

Miriam Gourley's appliqué method eliminates the need to press under the edges and prevents those inevitable burned fingers.

Instructions:

1. Cut out Lady Liberty Patterns on pages 93–95.

2. Cut out all designated felt pieces.

3. Place two pieces of print fabric for robe with right sides together and pin pattern piece to the fabric.

4. Using an old needle, carefully sew through the paper and the two layers of fabric, using a ⅛" seam allowance.

5. Pull away paper and immediately slit the top layer of fabric up the center, clip curves, trim corners, and turn the robe right side out. Press flat.

6. Repeat this procedure for the pieces of trim on the face, hands, robe, skirt, and socks. Use black thread to hand-stitch details on face. Paint cheeks with lipstick.

7. Assemble the figure on the pillow-front fabric, pin in place, and whipstitch onto pillow front.

8. Using all strands of floss in an embroidery needle, appliqué the shoes and embroider the stars onto the pillow top and the Xs around the edges.

9. Press one long edge of each 12" x 21" piece under ½", then press a 1½" hem and sew in place. In order to close the back with buttons, measure and sew button-holes and buttons.

10. Overlap the two hemmed edges until the back measures 21" sq. and sew together at each side. This will be the opening at the center back of the pillowcase for inserting the form.

11. Place the back and front pieces with right sides together and sew all edges, using a ½" seam allowance. Turn right side out and insert pillow form.

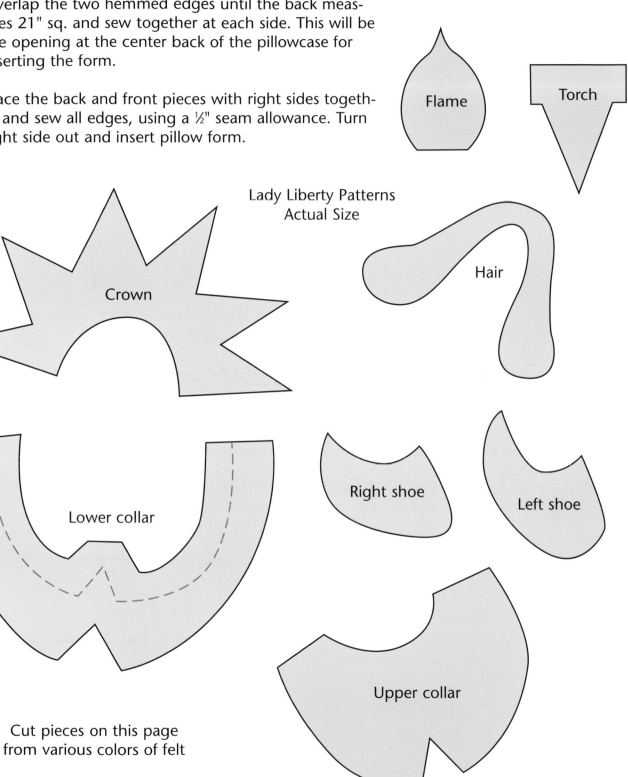

Flame

Torch

Lady Liberty Patterns
Actual Size

Crown

Hair

Lower collar

Right shoe

Left shoe

Upper collar

Cut pieces on this page
from various colors of felt

Face

Note: Feel free to add extra details in face, hands, or crown. This pattern was designed to be very simple.

Lady Liberty Patterns
Actual Size

Detail of stitching and pattern placement

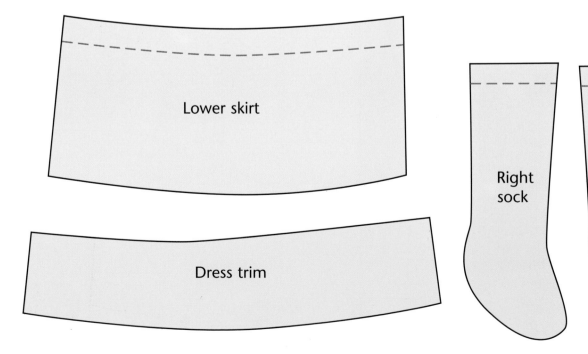

Lower skirt

Dress trim

Right sock

Left sock

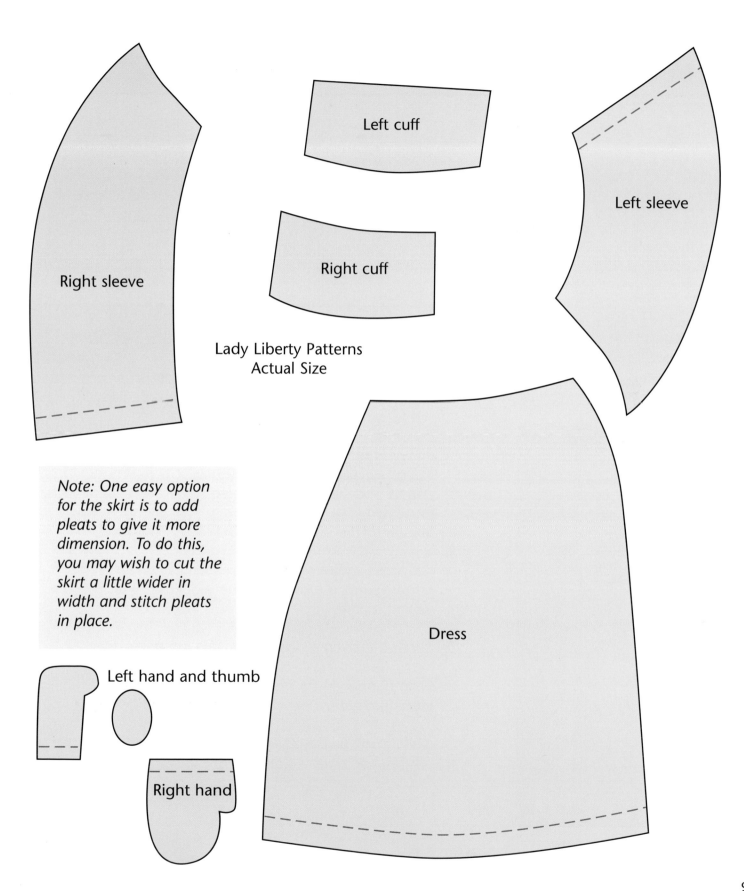

Left cuff

Left sleeve

Right cuff

Right sleeve

Lady Liberty Patterns
Actual Size

Note: One easy option for the skirt is to add pleats to give it more dimension. To do this, you may wish to cut the skirt a little wider in width and stitch pleats in place.

Dress

Left hand and thumb

Right hand

Faux Mola Panel

Supplies:

Cotton fabrics: black, red

Light-colored fabric-marking pen or pencil

Scraps of cotton: turquoise, yellow

White fabric-paint pen

Detail of faux mola stitching

The Cuna Indians stitch molas (reverse appliqué) into panels and to their blouses. Hmong needleworkers also use reverse appliqué in distinctive, intricate geometric designs like the piece pictured. The top layer is cut and stitched to reveal colored layers beneath. This project has been adapted for traditional appliqué techniques.

Instructions:

1. Cut the black fabric to 11" x 15" and the red fabric into ¾" strips as long as possible.

2. Fold and press under ¼" along each long edge of the red fabric.

3. Enlarge and transfer Mola Pattern from page 98 onto the black fabric back, using the light-colored marking pen to make lines where the red strips will be appliquéd.

4. Slip-stitch the edges of the red strips into place.

5. Cut small squares from the yellow and turquoise scraps. Stitch a turquoise square diagonally to a larger yellow square.

6. Stitch the layered squares to the faux mola panel.

7. Echo the geometrics of the stitching with the white fabric-paint pen and a ruler.

   Note: Don't be locked into just drawing lines; use dots, dashes, and small X's to highlight the panel.

Note: Molas can be made with as many as seven layers of fabric. Larger patterns are cut from the top piece and smaller patterns are cut from the successive layers. If an accent color is needed for only a small area, the fabric needed can be inserted in that area so as not to interfere with the other areas of the pattern.

Note: Modern-day molas also include surface embroidery to enhance the patterns.

Mola Pattern
Enlarge 150%

Table Runner

Supplies:

Cream embroidery floss

Khaki fabric: ¾ yd.

Muslin fabric: 2 yds.

Polyester fleece: 2 yds.

Rose fabric: ¾ yd.

A table runner is a cozy touch that gives class to any Christmas decor. Keep it simple and you can't go wrong.

Instructions:

1. Enlarge and cut out Leaf and Poinsettia Petal Patterns on page 101.

2. From muslin, cut two 18" x 72" pieces and from fleece, cut one 18" x 72" piece. Cut rounded corners on ends according to Figure 1.

3. Cut petals for one large and one small poinsettia from rose fabric.

4. Cut a bias strip 2" x 5 yd. from khaki fabric for use as a binding.

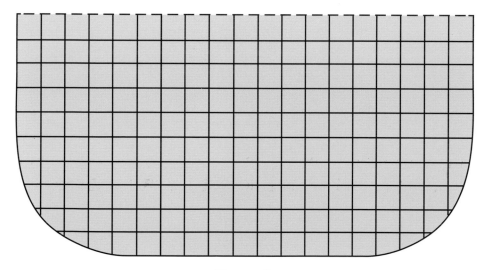

Figure 1
Each square = 1"

Tip: Plot out 1" squares on butcher paper using Figure 1 as a model. Find a large round object such as the bottom edge of a tin can or a saucepan lid and use it to trace the curve for each corner.

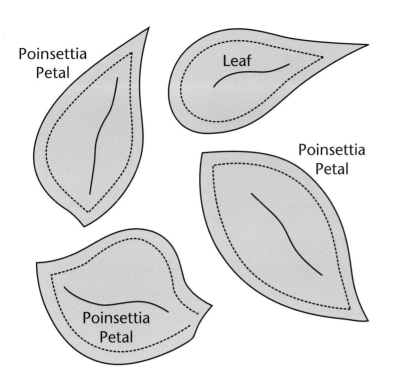

Poinsettia Petal

Leaf

Poinsettia Petal

Poinsettia Petal

Enlarge Patterns
200%

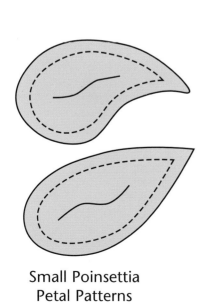

Small Poinsettia
Petal Patterns

5. Trim ¼" seam allowances from edges of each leaf and poinsettia pattern piece. Trace floral design onto one end of the muslin piece. See Figure 2.

6. Pin leaf or petal in place according Figure 2. Needle-turn the edge about ⅛" as you blind-stitch around the leaf.

7. Mark veins in leaves and petals. Blanket-stitch each vein with one strand of floss. Make twelve French knots in the center of each poinsettia, using two strands of floss wrapped around the needle twice.

8. Lay blank muslin wrong side up. Place fleece on top, followed by appliquéd muslin. Baste. Stitch binding to top side of runner with ⅜" seam allowance. Fold binding onto back of runner and slip-stitch into place.

9. Quilt as desired.

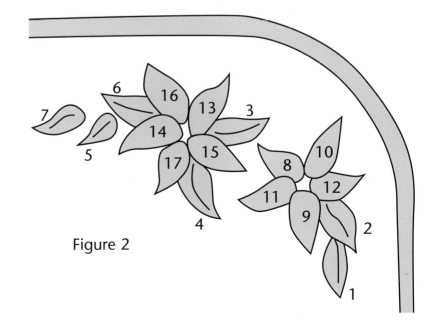

Figure 2

Patch-quilt Square

Traditional Scrapplique Design

Supplies:

Batting: ¼ yd.

Gingham flannel for backing: ¼ yd.

Scraps of fabrics in country colors and textures

Tip: By selecting colors that are more red and green, the wreath takes on a Christmas motif. Add small red circles for holly berries.

Tip: If flannel colors are too vivid, tea-stain fabric before adding batting and quilting. For tea-staining instructions, see Tea-stained Doily on page 108.

Need something to spice up a table display? Try this attractive quilt square, it is just right for any location.

Instructions:

1. Select eight scraps of fabric that go together well. Cut four pieces into 5½" squares. Cut each square diagonally twice, making sixteen triangles, each with one 5½" side.

2. Cut the other four pieces of fabric into 4½" squares, then cut each square diagonally twice.

3. Using the Patch-quilt Square Patterns, cut nine berry circles and nine leaf shapes from various scraps of fabric.

4. Stitch four different small triangles together to form a patchwork square.

5. Stitch larger triangles to long (outside) sides of square.

6. Appliqué berries and leaves to top of squares, referring to photo on page 103 as a guide for placement.

7. Layer backing and batting together and place the appliquéd square on top. Fold backing edges over to form binding. Stitch binding down.

8. Quilt as desired.

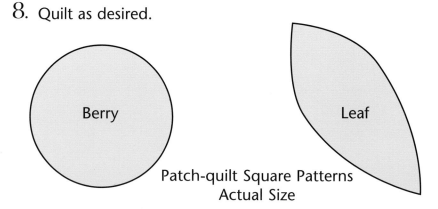

Berry

Leaf

Patch-quilt Square Patterns
Actual Size

Crazy-quilt Stockings

Supplies:

Purchased Christmas
stocking pattern

Embellishments: beads,
old jewelry, rhinestones

Metallic embroidery
flosses

Muslin: 1 yd.

Ribbon: 2" x ¼ yd.

Satin lining: 1 yd.

Scraps of fabrics: satins,
silks, velvets

Detail of crazy-quilt stitching

Want a one-of-a-kind gift for Christmas? Try giving a
crazy-quilt stocking—it's not just crazy, it's perfect.

Instructions:

1. Using a Christmas stocking pattern, cut two stockings
   from the muslin and two from the lining fabric.

2. Mark the stitching line on both muslin pieces. Lay the
   first fabric scrap on one of the muslin pieces in the
   top-left corner, making certain the fabric extends over
   the seam line.

3. Stitch the scrap to the muslin.

4. Fold ¼" edge of the next fabric scrap and place over
   the raw edge of the first piece. Appliqué in place.
   Continue until the entire piece of muslin is covered.
   Baste around the edges of the stocking. Repeat as
   above for the other muslin piece.

5. Embellish the seams of the stocking pieces with
   embroidery stitches and beads. Avoid placing beads in
   the seam line.

6. Sew around the edge of the stocking, with right sides
   together, leaving a ¼" seam allowance. Turn the stocking right side out.

7. Using a ¼" seam allowance, with wrong sides together,
   sew around the lining edge.

8. Slip the sewn lining into the stocking, matching up the
   tops. Fold both the lining and the stocking over ¼" and
   stitch the top.

Heirloom (air-loom) Scrappliqué — having
the appearance or quality of being kept
from one generation to another. Of timeless
value and general appeal.

Heirloom Scrappliqué

Tea-stained Doily

Heirloom Scrapplié Design

Supplies:

Button

Coffee or Tea

Doily

Pillow

Vinegar

Tip: Different teas make different hues:
  Coffee–warm brown
  Berry tea–pale pink
  Black tea–light tan
  Green tea–yellow

Note: This is a nice way to enjoy vintage doilies that were handed down from your mother or grandmother. The button could be from an old dress, earring, or broach.

One of the rewards of home decorating is to display a common item in a new and different way. Tea-staining gives a doily a warm, aged feel. Placing the doily on a pillow softly frames it and makes a wonderful accent for your room.

Instructions:

1. Select a natural-fiber or cotton/polyester-blend doily. Prewash and dry.

2. Heat a large pot of water to boiling and add ten tea bags or equivalent measure of coffee. Steep for 5–10 minutes.

   Note: Adding up to twenty bags of tea will make stain darker, but more than twenty bags will not make a significant difference in the color.

3. Submerge doily in tea bath. Allow to sit for *twenty* minutes. When desired color is achieved, add ½ cup vinegar to set the dye. Allow doily to sit in vinegar/tea solution an additional minute.

4. Remove doily and rinse in cool water.

5. Towel-dry, then permanently set the color by drying doily in dryer or by ironing until dry.

6. Appliqué doily onto a pillow.

7. Add vintage button to doily center.

Lace-trimmed Jacket

When my daughter dis-
carded a linen jacket, I
recycled it with the help
of some old crocheted
doilies.

Instructions:

1. Cut a small doily in
   half and zigzag-stitch
   the cut edges. Lay the
   doily onto the pocket
   and tuck the sewn
   edge inside. Hand-
   stitch it in place, then
   sew the doily along
   the outside edge of
   the pocket.

2. Use doilies large
   enough that when cut
   in half, zigzagged,
   and turned under
   could be sewn to the
   right and left sides of
   the collar and lapels in
   the same way as was
   done for the pocket.

Black Bedspread

Supplies:

Bedspread pattern

Black fabric: 9 yds.

Blue piping: 10½ yds.

Green fabric: 1½ yds.
(Or enough scraps for
leaves and stems.)

Scraps of cotton fabrics
for flowers and yo-yos

The black background and bright floral design on this bedspread makes a beautiful and dramatic decorating statement that lights up an entire bedroom.

Instructions:

1. Assemble the bedspread top according to the commercial pattern selected.

2. Using Bedspread Patterns on page 113, cut out stems and leaves from green fabric.

3. From various scraps of colored fabrics, cut out flowers and circles.

4. Using the fabric circles, make yo-yos. Run a gather stitch ⅛" in around the edge of the circle. Pull the thread to gather and secure the thread with a knot. Flatten the circle with the gathers in the center.

5. Lay out the remaining elements of the bedspread, starting with the stems and leaves. Appliqué the stems and leaves.

6. Appliqué the flowers and stitch a yo-yo in the center of each flower.

7. Add more yo-yos to the stems to represent unopened flowers.

8. Finish bedspread as instructed by bedspread pattern.

Detail of bedspread appliqué

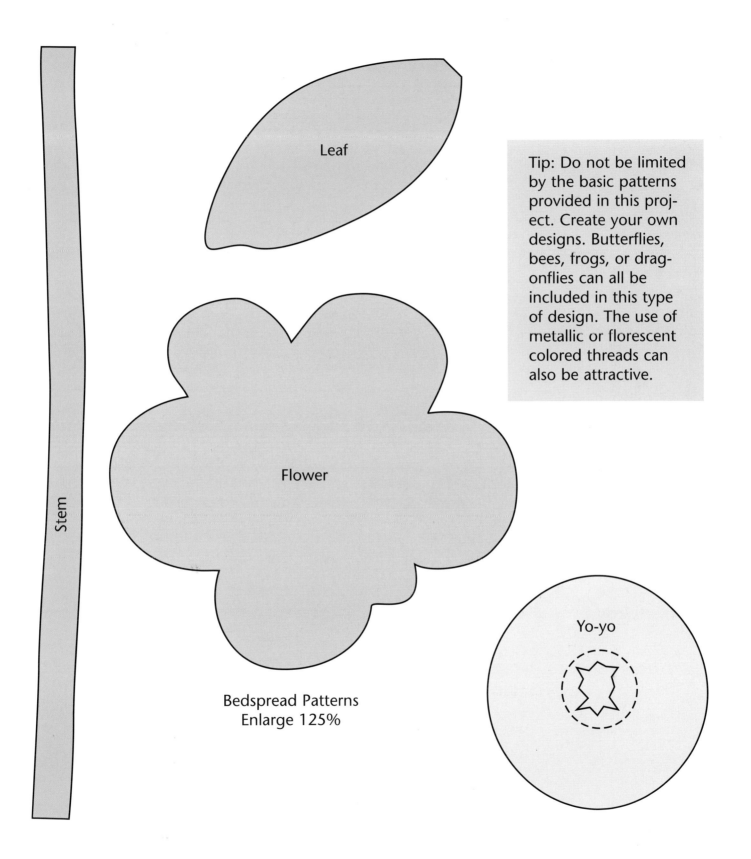

Leaf

Stem

Flower

Tip: Do not be limited by the basic patterns provided in this project. Create your own designs. Butterflies, bees, frogs, or dragonflies can all be included in this type of design. The use of metallic or florescent colored threads can also be attractive.

Bedspread Patterns
Enlarge 125%

Yo-yo

Pansy Doily

Supplies:

Embroidery flosses:
black, green, purple,
yellow

Fine linen fabric: ½ yd.
(Or purchase a premade
doily.)

Fusible web

Scraps of yellow fabric

It is getting difficult to find a really nice doily these days.
This particular pattern is not only easy, it is beautiful.

Instructions:

1. Cut out the Pansy Pattern from linen. Transfer the embroidery lines as indicated.

2. Iron the fusible web to the wrong side of the yellow scraps of fabric, following manufacturer's instructions. Cut out the pansy petals from the yellow scraps.

3. Starting with the bottom petal (the top left), lay the fabrics for the flower in the appropriate places.

4. Fuse the flower in place.

5. With the embroidery flosses, do blanket stitches around all the edges of the petals.

6. Embroider the remaining elements on the doily.

7. A crocheted edge can be added to the outer edge of the doily or it can be finished with a fine hem.

Pansy Pattern
Actual Size

Watercan Pillows

Designed by Tracy Merrill

Supplies:

Embroidery flosses:
blue, green, red

Fabric scraps

Muslin: ½ yd.

Pillow form: 18" sq.

White cotton: ½ yd.

The thing I like about crazy-quilting is it works up fast, you can duplicate the project again and again.

Instructions:

1. Cut an 18½" square from the muslin.

2. Appliqué the fabric scraps to the muslin in a crazy-quilt pattern. Edges of scrap may be turned under with a ¼" seam allowance or left flat to naturally fray, depending on the desired look of the finished piece.

3. Enlarge and transfer the watercan Pattern onto a selected fabric scrap and cut out. Once again, a seam allowance of ¼" may be added, or piece can be left to fray. Place on pillow top and stitch with flosses.

4. Select a contrasting scrap and cut out heart shape. Appliqué heart onto watercan.

5. Cut the white cotton fabric into an 18½" square.

6. Right sides together, sew the back of the pillow to the front, using a ¼" seam allowance.

7. Insert the pillow form and stitch the opening closed.

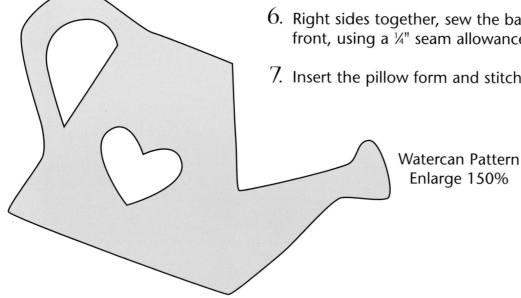

Watercan Pattern
Enlarge 150%

Lace Lid

Supplies:

3"-wide round black porcelain jar specially made for needlework

Dressmaker's pen

One decorative button

Seven styles of laces: white, cream, 2"–3" lengths

Three bugle beads to match button

Unbleached muslin: 4" sq.

Making a lace lid for a porcelain jar is a gift that is both delicate and useful.

Instructions:

1. Center and trace the acetate circle from the jar lid onto the muslin.

2. Arrange the lace in layers as desired, using the pen line as a guide. See Figure 1. Tack the lace edges to the muslin.

3. Stitch on button and beads.

4. Cut muslin and lace on the pen line. Complete lid according to manufacturer's instructions.

Figure 1

Ribbon Doll

Supplies:

Beads for eyes (optional)

Embroidery flosses or fabric markers

Fabric for body: ¼ yd., cotton print, plain or dyed muslin, or sturdy taffeta (Make use of fray preventive.)

Fabric glue (optional)

Polyester stuffing

Print fabric for hands and face

Scrap of velveteen for boots

Scraps of ribbons and embroidered trims

Tulle or net: 8" x 24"

Note: Use light- to medium-weight fabrics. Heavy fabrics will be too difficult to turn.

I had the delightful opportunity of working at the McCurdy Doll Museum off and on for almost 20 years. Oh, the inhabitants of that little Victorian house—and their stories! But that could be another book entirely. My favorites were the cloth dolls.

Instructions:

1. Cut out all Ribbon Doll Patterns on pages 121–123 from appropriate fabrics.

2. Lay face in center of head on one body piece. Satin stitch-around it. Machine- or hand-embroider features, or use fabric markers. Beads for eyes are optional.

3. Sew boot to end of lower-leg, right sides together. Press seam allowance open. Repeat for other leg.

4. Lay hand on end of arm, right sides together. Using ½" seam allowance, sew, then press seam allowance toward arm. Repeat for other arm.

5. Plan arrangements of ribbons and embroidered trims.

6. Sew trims across body, arms, and leg pieces. Occasionally use a zigzag stitch in a contrasting color on plain ribbon to add variety.

7. Sew a 3" ribbon tie at the top of each leg piece, at the bottom of each upper-leg piece, and the front body piece for each leg.

8. Sew a 5" ribbon tie at the top of each arm and on each side of the body at the shoulder.

9. Arrange 2" loops of ribbon around head from ear to ear, pinning in place to secure. Sew around edge of head to fasten ribbon.

10. Lay front to back, right sides together, and sew around body, leaving bottom open. Clip neck corners and turn.

11. Fold each arm and leg piece, right sides together, and sew, leaving an opening for stuffing. Be certain not to catch ribbons in seams. Turn.

12. Stuff all pieces with polyester stuffing. Turn open edges in ¼" and hand-stitch closed.

13. Tie lower- and upper-leg pieces together with a square knot (remember: right over left, left over right). Trim ribbon ends at an angle.

14. Tie upper legs to body in the same manner.

15. Tie arms to body and then tie bows.

   Note: A dab of glue will help hold the knots together.

16. Gather-stitch the long edge of the tulle. Cut a piece of embroidered trim to fit the doll's waist, adding 1½" for overlap. Adjust gathers to fit the waist, then sew the tulle to the trim.

17. Stitch snaps onto the waistband, or stitch waistband onto the doll.

Tip: This doll can be made from vintage fabrics with a skirt that is an old lace tablecloth or doily. She can also be made for Christmas by using fabrics that are shades of red and green for a country Christmas, or burgundy and evergreen for a more elegant Christmas gift or celebration.

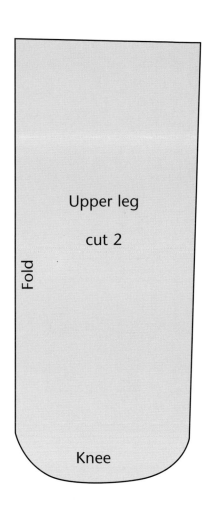

Upper leg

cut 2

Fold

Knee

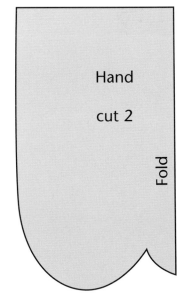

Hand

cut 2

Fold

Ribbon Doll Patterns
Actual Size

Ribbon Doll Patterns
Actual Size

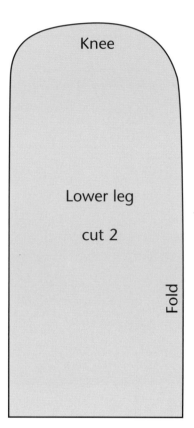

Knee

Lower leg

cut 2

Fold

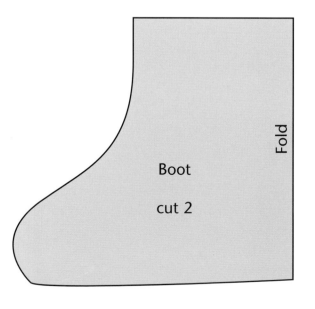

Boot

cut 2

Fold

Tip: A doll's face is a key element in making the doll look finished and attractive. Spend the time needed to draw and stitch the face.

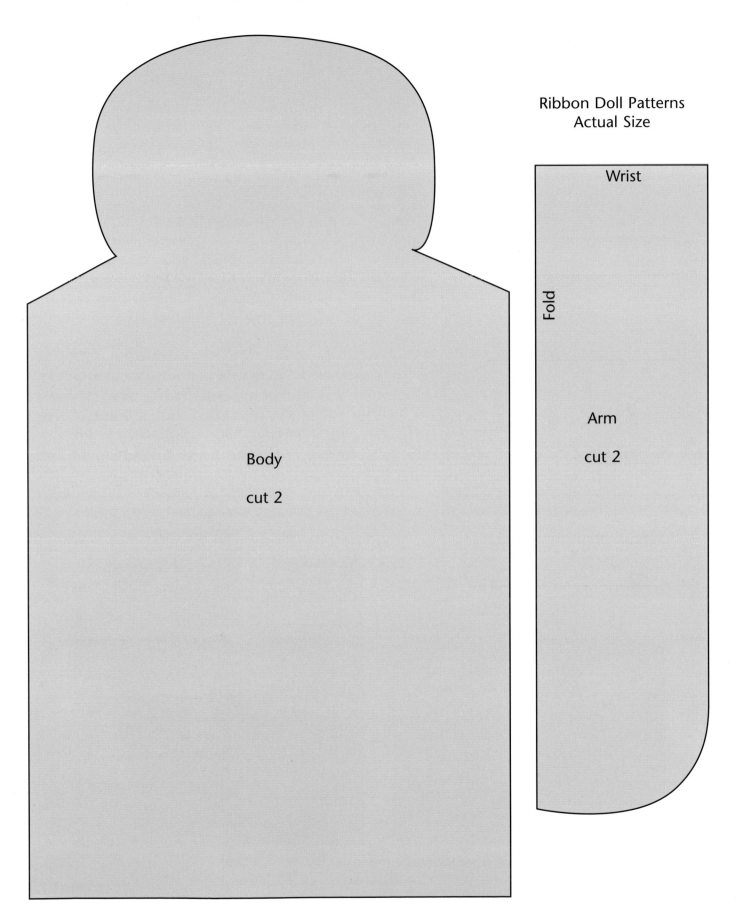

Ribbon Doll Patterns
Actual Size

Wrist

Fold

Arm

cut 2

Body

cut 2

123

Author Gallery

Author, Jean Marshall, was born in Salt Lake City, Utah; but moved to Inglewood, California, in time to start first grade. When Jean was eight years old, her mother taught her to sew on a little Singer® Featherweight®. Jean felt she had found her medium.

Jean majored in English at Cal State in L.A., then graduated in English from Brigham Young University. She continued her education at BYU and earned an M.A. in English. She married Don Marshall in 1963 and they have three children. Daughters, Robin and Jordan, and son, Reagan. Jordan and her husband Tyler have two children, Max and Lucy.

Jean has traveled and taught in many places around the world, but her home base is Provo, Utah. She was in her 50s before she attempted a major piece of wearable art, "My Utah Coat," and it ended up at the National Museum of Women's Art in Washington, D.C.

For the benefit of the reader, a selection of the author's work has been included on the next three pages.

"Shakespeare Vest," crazy patch made from scraps from the costume shop at the Utah Shakespearian Festival.

Above, "My Utah Coat," at right, "My Other Utah Coat." Small photos above right correspond left and right with the larger "Utah" coats' fronts.

Klimtomania - Patchwork coat in gold and silver lamé. This coat is inspired by motifs from the paintings of Gustav Klimt and includes photo transfers of Klimt, "The Kiss," and details from other paintings. Photographer, Leon Woodward.

Acknowledgments

I must gratefully acknowledge and thank my mother, Kay Stockseth, who taught me to knit and sew. First for my dolls, and then for myself. Her patience and praise, along with her gifts as a seamstress, remain my inspiration. I must also acknowledge my friend—an artist herself and my mentor—Sharon Gray. She urged me to take my first fiber class and she attended the birth of my first fiber piece, "My Utah Coat." I also owe thanks to my husband and children for their confidence and encouragement.

Jean Marshall

Special Contributors

Project contributor Miriam Gourley is a freelance designer. She has designed projects for Cranston Print Work's web site, V.I.P. Fabrics, and Concord House Fabrics, to name a few. She has taught doll-making and has copro-duced a television special.

Project contributor Tracy Merrill lives on a farm with her husband Jeff, six pug dogs, two cats, four llamas, and a flock of chickens. She enjoys making and collecting Santas, gardening, soap making, and hosting tea parties.

Project contributor Jenni Christensen is not actually a fabric artist, but loves any-thing made by hand. For twenty years her profession has been making floral etchings.

Project contributor Shauna Mooney Kawasaki has always been interested in art. She was the art director for a national children's magazine for 18 years. She has been involved in writ-ing, illustrating, and designing more than 20 books. She relaxes by sewing dolls for herself, her family, and for profit.

Index

Metric Equivalency Charts

Inches to Centimeters

inches	cm	inches	cm
⅛	0.3	6	15.2
¼	0.6	7	17.8
⅜	1.0	8	20.3
½	1.3	9	22.9
⅝	1.6	10	25.4
¾	1.9	11	27.9
⅞	2.2	12	30.5
1	2.5	13	33.0
1¼	3.2	14	35.6
1½	3.8	15	38.1
1¾	4.4	16	40.6
2	5.1	20	50.8
3	7.6	30	76.2
4	10.2	40	101.6
5	12.7	45	114.3

Yards to Meters

yards	meters	yards	meters
⅛	0.11	2	1.83
¼	0.23	2⅛	1.94
⅜	0.34	2¼	2.06
½	0.46	2⅜	2.17
⅝	0.57	2½	2.29
¾	0.69	2⅝	2.40
⅞	0.80	2¾	2.51
1	0.91	2⅞	2.63
1⅛	1.03	3	2.74
1¼	1.14	4	3.66
1⅜	1.26	5	4.57
1½	1.37	6	5.49
1⅝	1.49	7	6.40
1¾	1.60	8	7.32
1⅞	1.71	9	8.23